JAGUAR
4.2 LITRE 'E' TYPE
SERIES 2

JAGUAR CARS LIMITED, COVENTRY, ENGLAND

Telephone : ALLESLEY 2121 (P.B.X.)   Code BENTLEY'S SECOND   Telegrams : JAGUAR, COVENTRY   Telex 31622

Publication No. E.154/5

4.2 LITRE 'E' TYPE SERIES 2

FOREWORD

An owner is recommended to have operations not covered in this Handbook executed by the local Jaguar Distributor or Dealer, who is in a position to give authoritative advice and service. The satisfactory running and fine performance of which the car is capable, depends to a great extent upon the care and attention it receives from the owner. We, therefore, earnestly recommend that careful attention is paid to all instructions and that the servicing detailed in the "Routine Maintenance" section is carried out at the suggested periods. The text of the Handbook is divided into three sections:—

Operating Instructions

This section details the operation of the controls and equipment.

Routine Maintenance

This section lists specific items which should receive attention at prescribed mileage intervals.

Service Instructions

In this section maintenance instructions are detailed.
Additional information is given to assist the enthusiast or the owner living in a remote area where Jaguar service is not readily available.

North American Specifications

These vehicles are in full accordance with the U.S.A. Department of Health Requirements and produced to the Standard of Safety laid down in Federal Regulations for the U.S.A. and Canada.
Perusal of the handbook will indicate different carburetter equipment and attention is drawn to the important note on page 58. Axle ratios have been specifically chosen to suit the requirement of the North American market — see page 9.

Note

All references in this handbook to "right-hand side" and "left-hand side" are made assuming the person to be looking from the rear of the car or unit.

INDEX

CAR IDENTIFICATION

It is imperative that the Car and Engine numbers, together with any prefix or suffix letters are quoted in any correspondence concerning this vehicle. If the unit in question is the Gearbox the Gearbox number and any prefix or suffix letters must also be quoted. This also applies when ordering spare parts.

Car Number
Stamped on the right-hand frame cross member above the hydraulic damper mounting.

Engine Number (Early Cars)
Stamped on the right-hand side of the cylinder block above the oil filter and at the front of the cylinder head casting.

Engine Number (Later Cars)
Stamped on the crankcase bell housing flange on the left hand side of the engine adjacent to the oil dip stick.

8 or 9 following the engine number denotes the compression ratio.

FEDERAL SAFETY STANDARD CERTIFICATION PLATE

(U.S.A. CANADA ONLY)
Cars for the above countries will have a Certification plate attached to the left-hand door shut face. This contains the following information:-
Month/Year of Manufacture.
Commission Number.

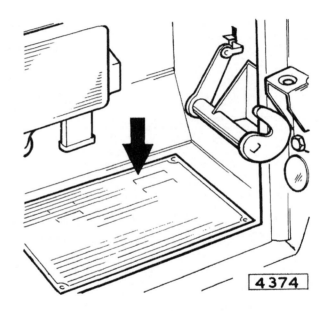

Fig. 1.   The identification numbers are also stamped on the plate indicated.

Gearbox Number
Stamped on a shoulder at the left-hand rear corner of the gearbox casing and on the top cover.

Automatic Transmission
Stamped on a plate attached to the Unit.

Body Number
Stamped on a plate attached to the right-hand side of the scuttle.

Key Numbers
The keys provided operate the ignition switch and door locks.

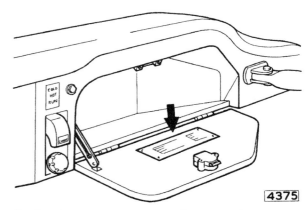

Fig. 2.   The tyre information plate (U.S.A. only)

IMPORTANT
These cars have Negative Earth (ground) systems and certain of the electrical components are different to those fitted to positive earth cars.

When fitting auxiliary equipment or replacing any of the electrical components use only those specified for this particular model.

TYRE INFORMATION
All cars sold in the U.S.A. will have a tyre information panel moulded in the wall of the tyre, necessary to conform to U.S.A. Federal Regulations. These panels give the following information:—
Maximum vehicle load
Maximum tyre pressures
A "Tyre Information Plate" attached to the glove box lid states:—

1—Vehicle capacity weight. 2—Designated seating capacity. 3—Designated seating distribution. 4—Recommended tyre pressures. 5—Recommended tyre size.

GENERAL DATA

Engine

Number of cylinders 6
Bore . . . . 3.625 in. (92.07 mm.)
Stroke . . . . 4.1732 in. (106 mm.)
Cubic capacity . . . . 4,235 c.c. (258.43 cu. ins.)
Compression ratio . . . . .8 to 1 or 9 to 1
Distributor contact breaker gap . . . . .014 in.—.016 in. (.36—.41 mm.)
Sparking plug type
   8 to 1 and 9 to 1 compression ratio . . . . Champion N.11Y
Sparking plug gap . . . . .025 in. (.64 mm.)
Ignition timing
   8 to 1 compression ratio . . . . 9 deg. B.T.D.C.
   9 to 1 compression ratio . . . . 10 deg. B.T.D.C.
Ignition timing (U.S.A. only) . . . . 5 deg. B.T.D.C. (Static)
                                        10 deg. B.T.D.C. (1,000 r.p.m.)

Valve Clearances (cold)	Inlet	Exhaust
Early cars	.004 in. (.10 mm.)	.006 in. (.15 mm.)
Later cars	.012 in.—.014 in. (.304—.355 mm.)	.012 in.—.014 in. (.304—.355 mm.)

Valve Seat Angle
   Inlet and Exhaust . . . . .45 deg.
Firing Order 1, 5, 3, 6, 2, 4
Tightening Torque Figures
   Flywheel . . . . 67 lb. ft. (9.2 kg. m.)
   Connecting rod . . . . 37 lb. ft. (5.1 kg. m.)
   Main bearings . . . . 83 lb. ft. (11.5 kg. m.)
   Cylinder head . . . . 50 lb. ft. (6.9 kg. m.)
   Camshaft bearings . . . . 9 lb. ft. (1.24 kg. m.)

Carburetters

Type: S.U. H.D.8 (triple)   STROMBERG 175 CD2SE (twin) (U.S.A. and Canada only)

Gearbox

Type: Four speed—synchromesh on 1st, 2nd, 3rd and top.
Type: Model 8 Automatic Transmission (2 + 2 only).

Front Suspension and Steering

Castor angle . . . . 2 deg. ± ½ deg. positive
Camber angle . . . . ¼ deg. ± ½ deg. positive
Front wheel alignment . . . . 1/16 in.—1/8 in. (1.6—3.2 mm.) toe-in

Rear Suspension

Camber angle . . . . ¾ deg. ± ¼ deg. negative

Final Drive

Type: Hypoid

Ratios
Standard Transmission U.S.A., Canada . . . . .3.54 : 1
Standard Transmission all other countries . . . . .3.07 : 1
Automatic Transmission (2 + 2 only, U.S.A. and Canada) . . . . . . .3.31 : 1
Automatic Transmission (2 + 2 only, all other countries) . . . . . . .2.88 : 1

Tyres

Tyre pressures (checked with tyres COLD)

	Front	Rear
Dunlop SP Sport 185VR15		
For speeds up to 125 m.p.h. (200 k.p.h.)	32 lb./sq. in. (2.25 kg./sq. cm.)	32 lb./sq. in. (2.25 kg./sq. cm.)
For speeds up to maximum . . . . *(Countries with no speed limitation)*	40 lb./sq. in. (2.81 kg./sq. cm.)	40 lb./sq. in. (2.81 kg./sq. cm.)

Tyres for Winter Use
(when snow conditions make the use of special tyres necessary)

Dunlop Weathermaster SP 44, 185 x 15
(For use only on rear wheels to replace SP. Sport tyres) . . . . 32 lb./sq. in.
(2.25 kg./sq. cm.)

Special inner tubes, identified by the tyre size and the wording "Weathermaster only", are available and **MUST** be fitted with these tyres.
Maximum permitted speed 100 m.p.h. (160 k.p.h.)

Capacities

	Imperial	U.S.	Litres
Engine (refill including filter)	15 pints	18 pints	8.5
Gearbox (Early cars)	2½ pints	3 pints	1.42
Gearbox (Later cars)	3 pints	3¼ pints	2.4
Automatic transmission unit from dry (2+2 only)	16 pints	19 pints	9
Final Drive Unit	2¾ pints	3¼ pints	1.54
Cooling system (including heater)	27 pints	32 1/5 pints	15.36
Petrol tank	14 gallons	16¾ gallons	63.64

Dimensions and Weights

Wheelbase (Open and fixed head coupe)	8 ft. 0 in. (2.44 m.)
(2 + 2)	8 ft. 9 in. (2.66 m.)
Track, Front	4 ft. 2 in. (1.27 m.)
Track, Rear	4 ft. 2 in. (1.27 m.)
Overall length (Open and fixed head coupe)	14 ft. 7 5/16 in. (4.45 m.)
(2 + 2)	15 ft. 4 7/16 in. (4.78 m.)
Overall width	5 ft. 5¼ in. (1.66 m.)
Overall height (Fixed head coupe)	4 ft. 0 1/8 in. (1.22 m.)
(Open 2 seater)	3 ft. 10½ in. (1.18 m.)
(2 + 2)	4 ft. 2 1/8 in. (1.27 m.)
Weight (dry) approximate (Fixed head coupe)	22½ cwt; (1123 kg.)
(Open 2 seater)	22 cwt. (1098 kg.)
(2 + 2 Standard transmission)	24½ cwt. (1245 kg.)
(2 + 2 Automatic transmission)	24¾ cwt. (1257 kg.)
Turning circle	37 ft. 0 in. (11.27 m.)
(2 + 2)	41 ft. 0 in. (12.19 m.)
Ground clearance	5½ in. (140 mm.)

Lamp Bulbs

LAMP	LUCAS BULB No.	VOLTS	WATTS	APPLICATION
Head	Sealed Beam Unit 410 411	12 12 12	75/45 50/40 45/40 45/40 (Yellow)	Home and R.H. Drive export L.H. Drive except Europe L.H. Drive European France
Side	989	12	6	Not Belgium, Germany, Holland, Switzerland
Front and Rear Flashing Indicators Reversing Light	382 273	12 12	21 21	
Rear/Brake	380	12	21/6	
Number Plate Illumination	207	12	6	
Interior Lights	382 989	12 12	21 6	Open 2 Seater Fixed Head Coupe and 2 + 2
Map Light	989	12	6	
Instrument Illumination: Headlamp warning light Ignition warning light Fuel level warning light Handbrake/Brake Fluid warning light Mixture control warning light Electrically heated backlight indicator light Traffic warning device indicator light	987	12	2	
Switch indicator strip Flashing indicator warning light	281	12	2	
Automatic transmission selector quadrant	281	12	2	2 + 2
Headlamp pilot lamp	989	12	6	Belgium, Germany, Holland, Switzerland

ROAD SPEED/R.P.M. DATA

The following tables give the relationship between engine revolutions per minute and road speed in miles and kilometres per hour.

The safe maximum engine speed is 5,500 revolutions per minute.

Engines must not, under ANY CIRCUMSTANCES, be allowed to exceed this figure.

It is recommended that engine revolutions **in excess of 5,000 per minute** should not be exceeded for long periods. Therefore, if travelling at sustained high speed on motorways, the accelerator should be released occasionally to allow the car to overrun for a few seconds.

Road Speed		Final Drive Ratio 3.31:1 Engine Revolutions Per Min.			
K.p.h.	M.p.h.	First Gear 9.71:1	Second Gear 6.31:1	Third Gear 4.6:1	Top Gear 3.31:1
32	20	2551	1658	1209	869
64	40	5100	3314	2416	1739
96	60		4972	3624	2608
128	80			4833	3477
160	100				4345

Note: The figures in these tables are theoretical and actual figures may vary slightly from those quoted due to such factors as tyre wear, pressures etc.

The safe maximum engine speed is 5,500 revolutions per minute.
Engines must not, under ANY CIRCUMSTANCES, be allowed to exceed this figure.
It is recommended that engine revolutions **in excess of 5,000 per minute** should not be exceeded for long periods.
Therefore, if travelling at sustained speed on motorways, the accelerator should be released occasionally to allow the car to overrun for a few seconds.

Road Speed		Final Drive Ratio 3.07:1 Engine Revolutions Per Min.				Final Drive Ratio 3.54:1 Engine Revolutions Per Min.			
K.p.h.	M.p.h.	First Gear 9.0:1	Second Gear 5.85:1	Third Gear 4.26:1	Top Gear 3.07:1	First Gear 10.39:1	Second Gear 6.74:1	Third Gear 4.92:1	Top Gear 3.54:1
32	20	2364	1537	1119	806	2729	1770	1292	930
64	40	4928	3073	2238	1613	5456	3541	2584	1860
96	60		4610	3357	2418		5311	3877	2789
128	80			4475	3225			5169	3718
160	100				4030				4647

Note: The figures in these tables are theoretical and actual figures may vary slightly from those quoted due to such factors as tyre wear, pressures etc.

AUTOMATIC TRANSMISSION DATA

2 + 2 only

Maximum ratio of torque convertor . . . . 2.00 : 1
1st gear reduction . . . . 2.40 : 1
2nd gear reduction . . . . 1.46 : 1
3rd gear reduction . . . . 1.00 : 1
Reverse gear reduction . . . . 2.00 : 1

Automatic Shift Speeds

185 VR 15 S.P. Sport Tyres 2.88 : 1 Final Drive Ratio
(all countries except U.S.A. and Canada)

Selector Position	Throttle Position	Upshifts		Downshifts		
		1—2	2—3	3—2	3—1	2—1
				M.P.H.		
D1	Minimum	7—9	12—15	8—14	—	4—8
	Full kickdown	52—56	81—89	73—81	20—24	20—24
D2	Minimum	—	12—15	8—14	—	—
	Full kickdown	—	81—89	73—81	—	—
L	Zero	—	—	ANY	—	12—20
				K.P.H.		
D1	Minimum	11—14	19—24	13—23	—	6—13
	Full kickdown	83—90	130—143	118—130	32—39	32—39
D2	Minimum	—	19—24	13—23	—	—
	Full kickdown	—	130—143	118—130	—	—
L	Zero	—	—	ANY	—	19—32

15

185 VR 15 S.P. Sport Tyres 3.31 : 1 Final Drive Ratio
(U.S.A. and Canada only)

Selector Position	Throttle Position	Upshifts		Downshifts		
		1—2	2—3	3—2	3—1	2—1
				M.P.H.		
D1	Minimum	6—8	11—13	7—13	—	3—7
	Full kickdown	45—49	70—78	63—71	17—21	17—21
D2	Minimum	—	11—13	7—13	—	—
	Full kickdown	—	70—78	63—71	—	—
L	Zero	—	—	ANY	—	10—18
				K.P.H.		
D1	Minimum	9—13	18—21	11—21	—	5—11
	Full kickdown	73—80	113—126	101—114	28—34	28—34
D2	Minimum	—	18—21	11—21	—	—
	Full kickdown	—	113—126	101—114	—	—
L	Zero	—	—	ANY	—	16—29

16

OPERATING INSTRUCTIONS

INSTRUMENTS

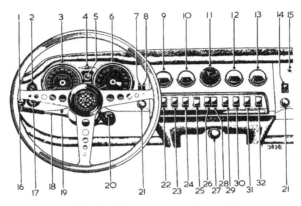

Fig. 3. Instruments and controls.

1. Headlamp dipper switch	17. Brake fluid/handbrake warning light
2. Heated rear window warning light	18. Flashing direction indicator and headlamp flasher switch
3. Speedometer	19. Speedometer trip control
4. Flashing direction indicator warning lights	20. Ignition/starter switch
5. Traffic hazard warning light	21. Air outlet controls
6. Revolution counter	22. Hazard warning switch
7. Heater — air control	23. Map light switch
8. Heater — temperature control	24. Interior light switch
9. Battery indicator	25. Panel light switch
10. Oil pressure gauge	26. Side light switch
11. Clock	27. Cigar lighter
12. Water temperature gauge	28. Headlight switch
13. Fuel contents gauge	29. Windscreen wiper switch
14. Choke control	30. Windscreen washer switch
15. Choke control warning light	31. Heater fan switch
16. Horn switch	32. Heated rear window switch

Battery Indicator

This is an instrument with a specially calibrated dial which indicates the condition of the battery. The position of the needle with a charged battery will be central within the area marked "Normal".

The instrument does NOT indicate the charging rate in amperes of the alternator.

Full instructions for reading the battery voltage by means of the meter are given on page 48.

Oil Pressure Gauge

The electrically operated pressure gauge records the oil pressure being delivered by the oil pump to the engine; it does not record the quantity of oil in the sump. The minimum pressure at 3,000 r.p.m. when hot should not be less than 40 lb. per square inch.

Note: After switching on, a period of approximately 20 seconds will elapse before the correct reading is obtained.

Water Temperature Gauge

The electrically operated water temperature gauge records the temperature of the coolant by means of a bulb screwed into the inlet manifold water jacket.

The instrument is divided into three segments — White, Normal and Red.

With the indicator in the White segment, the engine has not yet reached operating temperature; with the indicator in the Normal band, the engine is fully warmed up and is operating at the correct temperature. Should the indicator advance to the Red segment, the engine is overheating and the cause should be investigated immediately.

Fuel Level Gauge

Records the quantity of fuel in the supply tank. Readings will only be obtained when the ignition is switched "on".

Note: After switching on, a period of approximately 20 seconds will elapse before the correct reading is obtained.

Electric Clock (Early Cars)

The electric clock, fitted in the centre of the instrument panel, is fully transistorised and powered by a small dry battery. Frontal adjustment is provided by means of a knurled knob for setting the hands and a slotted screw for time keeping regulation.

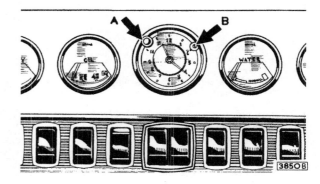

Fig. 4.   Clock controls.
A—Handsetting.
B—Time regulator.

To set the hands, pull the knob out, rotate and push in. To regulate the time keeping turn the slotted screw with a small screwdriver towards the positive sign (+) if gaining and the minus sign (−) if losing.

Electric Clock (Later Cars)

The electric clock fitted to later cars is a rectified instrument operated by the car battery and not by a mercury cell.

The time keeping and hand setting procedures remain unaltered.

Revolution Counter

Records the speed of the engine in revolutions per minute.

Speedometer

Records the vehicle speed in miles per hour, total mileage and trip mileage (kilometres on certain

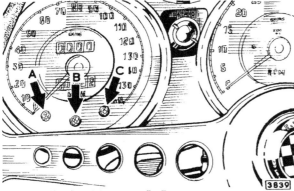

Fig. 5.　Warning lights.
　　　　 A—Ignition.
　　　　 B—Fuel.
　　　　 C—Headlamps main beam.

export models). The trip figures can be set to zero by pushing the winder upwards and rotating clockwise.

Headlamp Warning Light

A warning light marked "Headlamps" situated in the speedometer, lights up when the headlamps are in full beam position and is automatically extinguished when the lamps are in the dipped beam position.

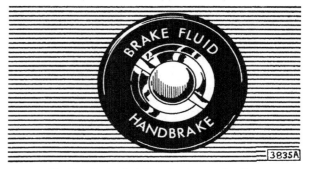

Fig. 6.　Brake fluid/handbrake warning light.

Ignition Warning Light

A red warning light (marked "ignition") situated in the speedometer lights up when the ignition is switched "on" and the engine is not running, or when the engine is running at a speed insufficient to charge the battery. The latter condition is not harmful, but always switch "off" when the engine is not running.

Fuel Level Warning Light

An amber warning light (marked "Fuel") situated in the speedometer lights up intermittently when the fuel level in the tank becomes low. When the fuel is almost exhausted the warning light operates continuously.

Flashing Indicator Warning Lights

The warning lights are in the form of green arrows located on the facia panel situated behind the steering wheel.

When the flasher indicators are in operation the arrow lights up on the side selected.

Brake Fluid Level and Handbrake Warning Light

A warning light (marked "Brake Fluid—Handbrake") situated on the facia behind the steering wheel, serves to indicate if the level in either of the two brake fluid reservoirs has become low, provided the ignition is "on". As the warning light is also illuminated when the handbrake is applied, the handbrake must be fully released before it is assumed that fluid level is low. If with the ignition "on" and the handbrake fully released the warning light is illuminated the brake fluid must be "topped-up" and the reason for the loss investigated and corrected immediately. IT IS ESSENTIAL that the correct specification of brake fluid be used when topping up.

As the warning light is illuminated when the handbrake is applied and the ignition is "on" a two fold purpose is served. Firstly, to avoid the possibility of driving away with the handbrake applied. Secondly, as a check that the warning light bulb has not "blown"; if on first starting up the car with the handbrake fully applied, the warning light does not become illuminated the bulb should be changed immediately.

CONTROLS AND ACCESSORIES

Accelerator Pedal
Controls the speed of the engine.
Brake Pedal
Operates the vacuum servo assisted disc brakes on all four wheels.
Clutch Pedal
On standard transmission cars connects and disconnects the engine and the transmission. Never drive with the foot resting on the pedal and do not keep the pedal depressed for long periods in traffic. Never coast the car with a gear engaged and clutch depressed.

Headlamp Dipper
Situated on the facia panel behind the steering wheel. The switch is of the "flick-over" type, and if the headlamps are on main beam, moving the lever will switch the dipped beam on, and main beam off. They will remain so until the switch lever is reversed.
Gear Lever (Standard Transmission Cars)
Centrally situated, and with the gear positions indicated on the control knob. To engage reverse gear first press the gear lever against the spring pressure before pulling the lever rearward. Always engage neutral and release the clutch when the car is at rest.

Automatic Transmission Selector Lever (2 + 2)
For full instructions on the operation of the automatic transmission, see page 35.

Handbrake Lever
Positioned centrally between seats. The handbrake operates mechanically on the rear wheels only and is provided for parking, driving away on a hill and when at a standstill in traffic. To apply the brake, pull the lever upward and the trigger will automatically engage with the ratchet. The handbrake is released by pressing in the knob, and pushing the lever downward.

Seat Adjustment
Both front seats are adjustable for reach. Push the lock bar, situated beside the inside runner, towards the inside of the car and slide into the required position. Release the lock bar and slide until the mechanism engages with a click.

To adjust the seat for rake, lift the lever situated on the outside of the cushion and adjust the seat back to the desired position.

On 2 + 2 cars, lift the lever and pull the squab forward to gain access to the rear seats.

Long-legged drivers who require the maximum amount of leg room, combined with the maximum rake of the seat back, may find it advantageous to locate the seat one notch forward from the rearmost position.

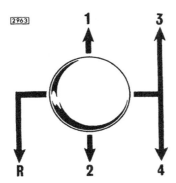

Fig. 7.   Gear positions.

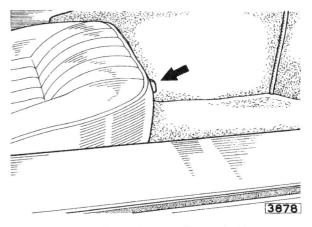

Fig. 8.   Seat adjustment (fore and aft).

21

Fig. 9.   Seat adjustment for rake.

Steering Wheel Adjustment

Rotate the knurled ring at the base of the steering wheel hub in an anti-clockwise direction two full turns when the steering wheel may be slid into the desired position. Turn the knurled ring clockwise to lock the steering wheel.

Door Locks

The doors may be opened from the outside by pressing the button incorporated in the door handles. Interior handles are recessed in a pocket which also incorporates a door pull.

To open, depress the handle: to lock lift the handle and allow to return to its normal position.

Both doors can be locked from the outside by means of the ignition key.

The locks are incorporated in the push buttons in the door handles.

To lock the right-hand door insert the key in the lock, rotate anti-clockwise as far as possible and allow the lock to return to its original position—the door is now locked.

To unlock the right-hand door turn the key clockwise as far as possible and allow the lock to return to its original position.

To lock the left-hand door rotate key clockwise; to unlock, rotate key anti-clockwise.

Fig. 10.   Steering wheel adjustment.

22

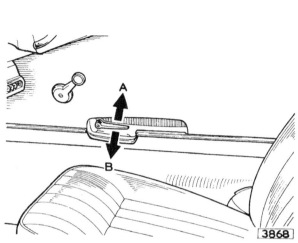

Fig. 11.   Door locks (internal).   A—to lock.   B—to open.

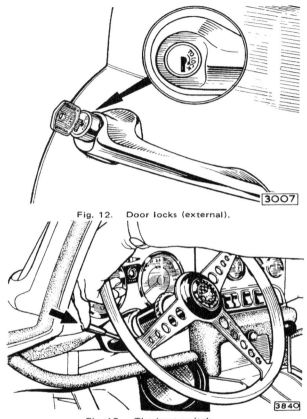

Fig. 12.   Door locks (external).

Fig. 13.   The horn switch.

Horn Switch

The horn switch is located in the direction indicator switch lever knob.

Switch the ignition ON and press the knob towards the steering column to operate the horns.

23

Ignition/Starter Switch (Early Cars)

Turn the key clockwise to position 3 (Fig. 14) to switch on the ignition and all ignition fused circuits. Press the key inwards and rotate clockwise to operate the starter motor. In this position (4) the ignition coil and petrol pumps will also be switched on. ALL other ignition controlled circuits will be momentarily switched OFF.

Release the key immediately the engine is firing to return to position (3). DO NOT operate the starter whilst the engine is running.

Turn the key anti-clockwise to position (1) to switch on Auxiliaries and ignition fused circuits. The ignition coil and petrol pumps will be switched "OFF".

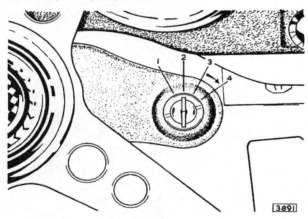

Fig. 14   The ignition/starter switch and steering column lock (early cars).

If your car is fitted with a combined Ignition/Starter Switch/Steering Column Lock the five position switch/lock is operated as follows:—

(1) Lock

This is the locked stop position. The key can be removed leaving the steering locked by engagement of the lock bolt with the register in the inner steering column.

(2) Park

This is the stop position. The key can be removed leaving the car capable of being steered with the ignition 'OFF'.

(3) Accessories

This position will allow the operation of accessories such as Radio (if fitted) with the ignition 'OFF'. The key cannot be removed.

(4) On

This is the driving position. The key cannot be removed and the ignition is 'ON'.

(5) Start

This is the starting position. On release the key will automatically return to the ignition 'ON' position.

Re-engagement of the starter (cranking) motor will not be possible until the key is returned to the 'park' position. This is a safety device introduced to prevent damage to the starter drive through accidental engagement when the engine is running.

IMPORTANT:
The steering column lock is brought into action when the key is turned to the lock position and then removed.

IMMEDIATELY THIS IS DONE IT BECOMES IMPOSSIBLE TO STEER THE CAR.

It is, therefore, important to remember, that if the ignition is switched off whilst the car is in motion, the key should not be turned past the "PARK" position (two clicks to the left).

THE IGNITION KEY SHOULD NEVER BE REMOVED FROM THE LOCK WHILST THE CAR IS MOVING.

Ignition/Starter Switch (Later Cars)

The ignition/starter switch also functions as a steering column lock.

The switch has three operative positions which are illustrated below.

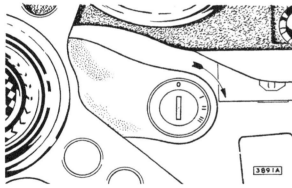

Fig. 15. The ignition/starter switch and steering column lock (later cars).

Operation

O — This is the 'OFF' position. Withdrawing the key when in this position will allow the steering column lock to operate by engagement of the lock bolt with the register in the inner column. It should be noted that the anti-theft device operates only when the key is turned to the 'OFF' position and removed.

IMMEDIATELY THIS IS DONE, THE COLUMN IS LOCKED AND IT BECOMES IMPOSSIBLE TO STEER THE CAR.

It is, therefore, important to remember that if the ignition is switched 'OFF' **THE IGNITION KEY SHOULD NEVER BE REMOVED FROM THE LOCK WHILST THE CAR IS MOVING.** Re-inserting the key will unlock the column.

I — This position will allow the operation of accessories such as Radio (when fitted) with the ignition switched 'OFF'.
The key cannot be removed.
Do not leave the car with the ignition key in this position.

II — This is the driving position. The key cannot be removed and the ignition is 'ON'. Do not leave the key in this position for any length of time with the engine stationary.

III — This is the starting position. On release the key will automatically return to the ignition 'ON' position (II).

IMPORTANT

Operation of the starter switch will momentarily isolate ALL IGNITION controlled equipment (except Coil and Petrol Pump) including Air Conditioning system (when fitted) allowing full battery power to be available for engine cranking.

KEY ALARM (U.S.A. AND CANADA)

In addition to the operations detailed above, the switch has an additional feature incorporated for U.S.A. and CANADA only to conform to U.S.A. Federal Regulations, known as Key Alarm.

In operation, a warning buzzer will sound whenever the driver's door is opened if the ignition key has been left in the lock.

Removal of the key will disconnect the buzzer.

Instrument Panel Switches

All switches are of the rocker type.

To switch "ON" press at the bottom.

To switch "OFF" press at the top.

Interior Light Switch

Operate the switch (marked "Interior") on the indicator strip to illuminate the driving compartment.

Lighting Switch

Side and headlamps may be illuminated simultaneously by operating the headlamp switch only. They may also be switched off together by switching off the sidelamp switch.

Head and sidelamp switches may be operated independently.

Panel Light Switch

Operate the switch lever (marked "Panel") to enable the instruments to be read at night and to provide illumination of the switch markings. The switch has two positions "Dim" and "Bright" to suit the driver's requirements. The panel lights will only operate when the side lights are switched on.

Map Light

Operate the switch lever (marked "Map") to illuminate the lamp situated above the instrument panel. To provide ease of entry into the car at night the map light is switched on when either one of the doors is opened, and is extinguished when the door is closed.

Flashing Direction Indicator

The "flashers" are operated by a lever behind the steering wheel. To operate the flashing direction indicators on the right-hand side of the car, move the lever clockwise; to operate the left-hand side indicators move the lever anti-clockwise. While the flashing indicators are in operation, the warning light on the facia panel behind the steering wheel will flash on the side selected.

Fig. 16. Flashing direction indicator control.

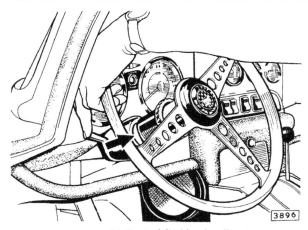

Fig. 17.   Method of flashing headlamps.

Headlamp Flasher

To "flash" the headlamps as a warning signal, lift and release the flashing indicator lever in quick succession. The headlamps can be "flashed" when the lights are "off" or when they are in the dipped beam position; they will not "flash" in the main beam position.

Braking Lights

Twin combined tail and brake lights automatically function when the footbrake is applied.

Luggage Compartment Illumination

The luggage compartment is illuminated by the interior light when this lamp is switched on.

Mixture Control Warning Light

A red warning light situated above the mixture control on the facia panel serves to indicate if the choke is in operation. This warning light is illuminated immediately the control lever is moved from "off" position.

To change the bulb, accessible behind the facia panel, pull bulb holder away from "clip in" attachment, and unscrew bulb by turning anti-clockwise. For full instructions on the use of the mixture control see "Starting and Driving" page 33.

Cigar Lighter

To operate, press holder (marked "Cigar") into the socket. On reaching the required temperature, the holder will return to the extended position. Do not hold the lighter in the "pressed-in" position.

Windscreen Wipers

The wipers are controlled by a three position switch (marked "Wiper"). Press the switch to the second position (Slow) which is recommended for all normal adverse weather conditions and snow. For conditions of very heavy rain and for fast driving in rain press the switch to the third position (Fast). This position should not be used in heavy snow or with a drying windscreen, that is, when the load on motor is in excess of normal, the motor incorporates a protective cut-out switch which under conditions of excessive load cuts off the current supply until normal conditions are restored.

When the switch is placed in the "Off" position the wipers will automatically return to a position along the lower edge of the screen.

Note: The wiper blades are manufactured with special anti-smear properties. Renew only with genuine Jaguar parts.

Windscreen Washer
For full instructions on the use of Windscreen Washing Equipment see page 28.

Heating and Ventilating Equipment
For full instructions on the use of the Heating and Ventilating Equipment see page 25.

Bonnet Lock
To open the bonnet turn the two small levers located on the right and left-hand door hinge posts anti-clockwise and pull to full extent. This will release the bonnet which will now be retained by the safety catch.

Insert the fingers under the rear edge of the bonnet and press in the safety catch.

To close the bonnet, ensure that the levers are pulled out to their full extent, push down to the safety catch position, push in the two levers and turn clockwise.

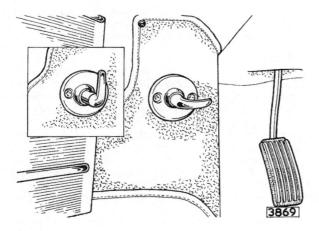

Fig. 18. Showing the bonnet lock lever in the locked position. The inset shows the lever in the unlocked position.

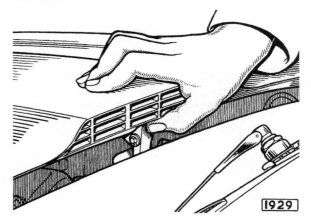

Fig. 19. Bonnet safety catch. (Open 2-seater and Fixed Head Coupe)

Driving Mirror Adjustment

The driving mirror, attached to the windscreen by a plastic screw which is designed to shear under impact, may be dipped for night time driving by pushing the separated portion at the bottom centre. For daytime driving, pull the centre portion rearwards.

Fuel Tank Filler

The fuel tank filler is situated in a recess in the left-hand rear wing and is provided with a hinged cover.

Tools

The tools are contained in a tool roll placed in the spare wheel compartment.

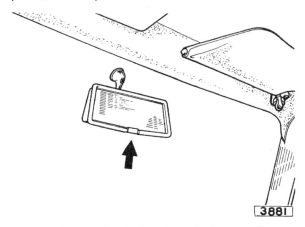

Fig. 20.   Interior driving mirror dipping operation.

Spare Wheel Jacking Equipment

The spare wheel is housed in a compartment under the luggage boot floor, and is accessible after removal of the square lid.

The copper hammer and jack are retained in clips in the luggage boot.

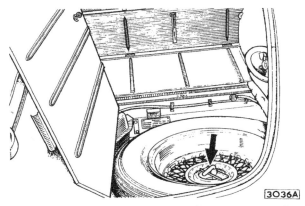

Fig. 21.   Spare wheel housing (Fixed head coupe).

Luggage Compartment (Open 2 Seater)

The luggage compartment is unlocked by turning the key in the direction of arrow "A" (Fig. 23) and pulling the lock barrel outwards in the direction of the arrow "B".

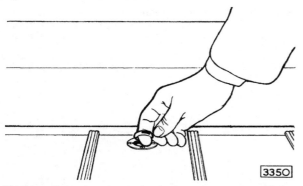

Fig. 22.   Removing the spare wheel compartment lid (2+2).

Luggage Compartment (Fixed Head Coupe and 2 + 2)
The luggage compartment is unlocked by lifting the recessed chromium plated lever situated in the body trim panel beside the right-hand seat. To operate, insert finger and lift out the lever to the full extent. The lid will now be retained in position by the safety catch.

Insert the fingers under the right-hand edge of the lid and press in the safety catch.
The lid is retained in the open position by means of a self-locking stay.

Fig. 23.   Luggage compartment lock control (Open 2 seater).

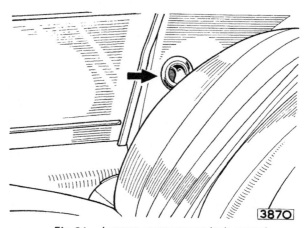

Fig. 24.   Luggage compartment lock control.

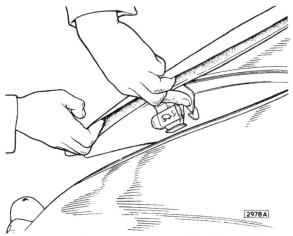

Fig. 25.   Luggage compartment lid safety catch.

SEAT BELTS
Anchorage points for seat belts are incorporated in the construction of the car. Approved belts should be fitted by an Authorised Distributor or Dealer.

Seat Back Panel (Fixed Head Coupe)
The back panel behind the seat normally serves as a partition behind the driving and luggage compartment. The panel can be lowered to give an increased boot floor area if required for extra storage.

To lower release the two side fixing bolts and drop panel forward. Stop arms should be raised to prevent luggage contacting back of seats. Return panel to vertical position when extra boot space is not required.

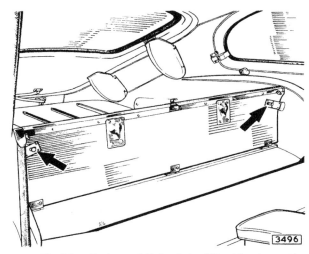

Fig. 26.   Back panel fixing bolts (Fixed head coupe).

31

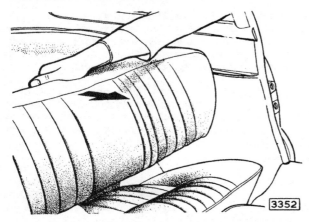

Fig. 27.   Moving the rear seat squab forward.

Rear Seat Squab (2 + 2)

The rear seat squab normally serves as a partition between the driving and luggage compartments. The top section of the squab can be hinged forward to give an increased luggage compartment floor area if required for extra stowage.

Traffic Hazard Warning Device (if fitted)

The traffic hazard warning system operates in conjunction with the four flashing turn indicator lamps fitted to the car and the operation of a switch on the instrument panel will cause these four lamps to flash simultaneously.

A red warning lamp is incorporated in the circuit to indicate that the hazard warning system is in operation.

Fig. 28.   Traffic hazard warning device.
A—switch.
B—warning light.

Electrically Heated Backlight (Optional Extra)

An electrically heated backlight to provide demisting and defrosting of the rear window is available as an optional extra.

32

A heating element, consisting of a fine wire mesh between the laminations of glass, is connected to the wiring harness and functions only when the ignition and heater switches are in the "ON" position.

An amber warning lamp, situated on the facia panel, lights up when the backlight heater is switched on. A resistance in the circuit through the side and headlamp switch automatically dims the warning lamp for night driving.

Fig. 29.   Backlight heater.
A—switch.
B—warning light.

STARTING AND DRIVING

Prior to Starting
Ensure that the coolant level and the engine oil level are correct. Check for sufficient petrol in the tank.

Starting from Cold
A manual mixture control (choke) is located in a recess on the right hand side of the facia panel. The control has six positions.
Pulling the lever fully outwards gives the "fully rich" mixture condition—indicated by "COLD" on the panel.
Progressively pushing in the lever weakens the mixture strength.
The two positions from "HOT" give a fast idle condition.
With the choke lever fully home ("RUN") the mixture strength is governed by the carburetter setting.
A red warning light is incorporated in the control which lights up immediately the lever is moved from "RUN" position.
When starting from cold the mixture control should be moved to the fully rich "COLD" position. Switch on the ignition and operate the starter switch, but do not touch the accelerator. Release the starter switch as soon as the engine fires—this is important. If for any reason the engine does not start do not operate the starter switch again until both the engine and starter motor have come to rest.
As soon as the engine speed increases slide the control progressively to the intermediate "HOT" position.

33

Always return the control to "RUN" position as soon as possible. Unnecessary use of the mixture control will result in reduced engine life and increased fuel consumption.

Starting in Moderate Temperature

In warm weather or if the engine is not absolutely cold, it is usually possible to start the engine with the mixture control in one of the intermediate "HOT" positions. Do not touch the accelerator pedal.

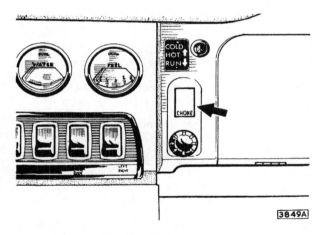

Fig. 30.   Choke control.

Starting When Hot

Do not use the mixture control. If the engine does not start immediately slightly depress the accelerator pedal when making the next attempt.

Warming up

Do not operate the engine at a fast speed when first started but allow time for the engine to warm up and the oil to circulate. A thermostat is incorporated in the cooling system to assist rapid warming up. In very cold weather run the engine at 1,500 r.p.m. with the car stationary until a rise in temperature is indicated on the temperature gauge.

Driving

(a)   Careful adherence to the "Running-in" Instructions given will be amply repaid by obtaining the best performance and utmost satisfaction from the car.

(b)   The habit should be formed of reading the oil pressure gauge, water temperature gauge and battery indicator occasionally as a check on the correct functioning of the car. Should an abnormal reading be obtained an investigation should be made immediately.

(c)   On standard transmission cars always start from rest in first gear; to start in a higher gear will cause excessive clutch slip and premature wear. Never drive with a foot resting on the clutch pedal and do not keep the clutch depressed for long periods in traffic.

(d)   The synchromesh gearbox provides a synchronized change in all forward gears. When changing down a smoother gear change will be obtained if the accelerator is left depressed to provide the higher engine speed suitable to the lower gear. Always fully depress the clutch pedal when changing gear.

(e) Gear changing may be slightly stiff on a new car but this will disappear as the gearbox becomes "run in".

(f) Always apply the footbrake progressively; fierce and sudden application is bad for the car and tyres. The handbrake is for use when parking the car, when driving away on a hill and when at a standstill in traffic.

"Running-in" Instructions

Only if the following important recommendations are observed will the high performance and continued good running of which the Jaguar is capable be obtained.

During the "running-in" period do not allow the engine to exceed the following speeds and particularly do not allow the engine to labour on hills; it is preferable to select a lower gear and use a higher speed rather than allow the engine to labour at low speed:—

First 1,000 miles (1,600 km.) . . . . . 2,500 r.p.m.
From 1,000—2,000 miles
(1,600—3,200 km.) . . . . 3,000 r.p.m.

Have the engine sump drained and refilled as recommended at the free service, that is, after the first 1,000 miles (1,600 km.).

AUTOMATIC TRANSMISSION (2+2)

Operation

The automatic transmission incorporates an hydraulic torque converter in place of the flywheel and clutch. This converter is coupled to an hydraulically operated planetary gearbox which provides three forward speeds and a reverse.

Operation of the automatic transmission is controlled by the driver through the selector lever mounted centrally in the console.

The quadrant markings, from front to rear, are P, R, N, D2, D1, L.

The selector lever can be moved freely between N and D2. To move the lever between D2 and D1, D1 and L, or to the P or R positions, the control lever must be pressed to the right against the spring pressure.

Warning

The handbrake or footbrake should be fully applied before selecting any of the forward drive ranges or reverse from a stationary position.

P (Park)

In the park position the gearbox is mechanically locked by means of the parking pawl which engages with external teeth formed on the ring gear integral with the driven shaft.

Park should **not** be selected when the car is in motion.

Use of the Park position is recommended whenever the car is parked with or without the engine running.

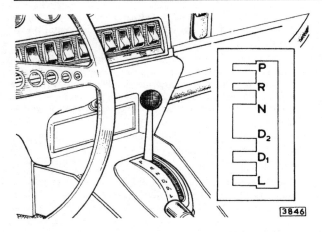

Fig. 31.   The automatic transmission selector.

R (Reverse)

The "R" position provides reverse ratio. Do not select Reverse when the car is moving forward.

N (Neutral)

All clutches are disengaged and there is no drive beyond the torque converter. The handbrake must be applied whenever Neutral is selected and the car is at rest.

D2 (Drive range, 2nd gear start)

In the Drive 2 position, the car starts from rest in second gear and operates automatically between second and third gears.

At, or below, a preset maximum vehicle speed, downshifts from 3rd to 2nd may be effected by depressing the accelerator fully. ("Kickdown" position).

First gear is not obtainable in this position but D2 is suitable for normal driving where maximum acceleration is not required.

In this position, the car will not roll back on hills as long as the engine is running.

D1 (Drive range, 1st gear start)

When in the D1 position, the car starts from rest in first gear and operates automatically through all three forward ratios. Upshifts and downshifts occur in accordance with car speed and throttle position.

At, or below, preset maximum road speeds downshifts may be effected from 3rd to 2nd, from 2nd to 1st, or, directly, from 3rd to 1st. This is accomplished by depressing the accelerator fully. ("Kickdown" position).

L (Lockup)

Lockup position provides overriding control for either first or second gear with engine braking in either ratio.

When starting from rest in the lockup position the transmission starts in 1st gear and remains in that gear regardless of road speed or throttle position.

Maximum engine braking is available in this gear. In either D1 or D2 with the transmission in 3rd gear, the selection of L will cause an immediate downshift to second gear. This will provide moderate engine braking when the throttle is closed.

If the road speed is reduced to approximately 16 m.p.h. (25 k.p.h.) the transmission will downshift automatically from second to first and provide maximum engine braking.

Once first gear is attained, no upshift will be possible until the selector lever is removed from the L position.

Starting

A starter inhibitor switch ensures that the starter will operate only when the selector is in either the P or N position.

Engine Braking

When engine braking is required whilst descending steep hills apply the footbrake to reduce speed to approximately 60 m.p.h. (96 k.p.h.) or below.

Move the selector lever to the L position to obtain an immediate downshift to second gear.

If the road speed is below 16 m.p.h. (25 k.p.h.) when L is selected the downshift will be directly from 3rd to 1st gear.

Rocking the Car

In order to extricate a car from mud, sand or snow, employ a constant slight throttle opening and rock the car backwards and forwards by alternately selecting the R and D2 positions.

Stopping

To bring the car to rest, release the accelerator and apply the brakes.

The selector lever may be left in L, D2, or D1 unless the car is to be parked.

Parking

When the car is stationary select the P (Park) position.

Push Starting

It is possible to effect an engine start by pushing the car.

To do this, select N and switch the ignition ON. Depress accelerator pedal approximately 1/3 and when the car reaches approximately 20 m.p.h. (32 k.p.h.) select D2 or L. Do NOT tow the car to start the engine—it may overtake the towing vehicle.

Towing

The car may be towed with a dead engine in an emergency. Before towing ensure that the transmission fluid is at the correct level. Towing should be done with the transmission selector in the N position and speed should not exceed 30 m.p.h. (48 k.p.h.).

If the car is being towed because of transmission damage, the propeller shaft should be removed or towing should be done by lifting the rear wheels from the ground. Failure to do this may result in further extensive transmission damage.

WHEEL CHANGING

Whenever possible the wheel changing should be carried out with the car standing on level ground, and in all cases with the handbrake fully applied. Unlock the luggage compartment as detailed previously.

The spare wheel is housed in a compartment underneath the luggage boot floor; the wheel changing equipment is retained in clips.

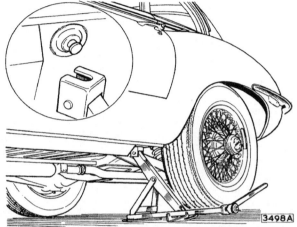

Fig. 33.   Jacking the 2+2 at the rear.

Fig. 32.   The jack in position for raising the right-hand side of the car.   (Fixed head coupe).

Place the hub cap removal tool over the hub cap. Using the mallet supplied in the tool kit, slacken but do not remove the cap; the caps are marked Right (off) side or Left (near) side, and the direction of rotation to remove is indicated by arrows.

The jacking sockets on open and fixed head coupe cars will be found centrally located on either side of the car.

On 2 + 2 cars four jacking pegs (two per side) are provided for raising the car.

The lifting pad of the jack is forked (inset, Fig. 33) and care must be taken to ensure that the fork is *fully located* on the peg before raising the car. The position of the lever (inset, Fig. 32) controls the operation of the jack screw for raising or lowering the car.

Place jack under car to locate in the socket (or peg) and raise car until wheels are clear of ground. Remove hub cap and withdraw wheel. Mount the spare wheel on the splined hub. Refit the hub cap and tighten as much as possible by rotating cap in the required direction, that is anti-clockwise for the right-hand side and clockwise for the left-hand side. Lower the jack and finally tighten the hub fully with the copper and hide mallet.

For cars fitted with pressed spoke wheels (optional extra), remove the nave plate by levering off with the special tool provided in the tool roll. Using the wheelbrace, loosen but do not remove the five wheel nuts. Raise the car on the jack until the wheel is well clear of the ground.

Remove the wheelnuts and withdraw the wheel from the studs.

Mount the spare wheel on the five studs and run up the nuts as tight as possible.

Lower the jack. Finally tighten all securing nuts.

Fit the nave plate over two of the three mounting posts and secure with a sharp tap of the hand at a point in line with the third post.

Fig. 34.   Hub cap—right (off) side.

39

FROST PRECAUTIONS

Anti-freeze—Important

During the winter months it is strongly recommended that an anti-freeze compound with an **inhibited Ethylene Glycol base**, such as Smith's "Bluecol", be used in the proportions of 50% solution for U.S.A. and Canada, 40% solution for all other countries.

It should be remembered that if anti-freeze is not used or is not of sufficient strength it is possible owing to the action of thermostat for the radiator to "freeze-up" whilst the car is being driven even though the water in the radiator was not frozen when the engine was started.

Before adding anti-freeze solution the cooling system should be cleaned by flushing. To do this, open the radiator block and cylinder block drain taps and insert a water hose into the radiator filler neck. Allow the water to flow through the system, with the engine running at 1,000 r.p.m. to cause circulation, until the water runs clear. The cylinder head gasket must be in good condition and the cylinder head nuts pulled down correctly, since if the solution leaks into the crankcase a mixture will be formed with the engine oil which is likely to cause blockage of the oil-ways with consequent damage to working parts. Check tightness of all water hose connections, water pump and manifold joints. To ensure satisfactory mixing, measure the recommended proportion of water and anti-freeze solution in a separate container and fill the system from this container, rather than add the solution direct to the cooling system.

Check the radiator water level after running the engine and top up if necessary. Topping up must be carried out using anti-freeze solution or the degree of protection may be lost. Topping up with water will dilute the mixture possibly to an extent where damage by frost will occur.

Engine Heater

Provision is made on the right-hand side of the cylinder block for the fitment of an American standard engine heater element No. 7, manufactured by "James B. Carter Ltd., Electrical Heating and Manufacturing Division, Winnipeg, Manitoba, Canada" or "George Bray & Co. Ltd., Leicester Place, Blackman Lane, Leeds 2, England".

Cars sold in Canada will have the engine heater fitted as standard equipment.

Warning

The fitting of an engine heater does not obviate the use of "anti-freeze" during the winter months.

CAR HEATING AND VENTILATING EQUIPMENT

Car Heating and Ventilating System

The car heating and ventilating equipment consists of a heating element and an electrically driven fan mounted on the engine side of the bulkhead. Air from the heater unit is conducted:

(a) To a built in duct situated behind the instrument panel.

(b) To vents at the bottom of the windscreen to provide demisting and defrosting.

The amount of fresh air can be controlled at the will of driver and is introduced into the system by operating the "Air" control lever and switching on the fan.

Air Control

The air control (A, Fig. 35) (marked "ON-AIR-OFF") controls the amount of fresh air passing through the heater element; when this control is placed in the "OFF" position the supply of air is completely cut off.

Placed in the "ON" position the maximum of air passes through the heater element. By placing the control in intermediate positions varying amounts of air may be obtained.

Temperature Control

The temperature control (B, Fig. 35) (marked "HOT—COLD") situated on the facia panel operates a valve which controls the amount of hot water passing through the heater element; when this control is placed in the "COLD" position the supply of hot water to the element is completely cut off so that cold air only can be admitted for ventilating the car in hot weather.

Placed in the "HOT" position the maximum amount of hot water passes through the heater element. By placing the control in intermediate positions varying degrees of heat may be obtained.

Air Distribution

The demisting outlets operate when the system is working, the outlets under the duct behind the instrument panel should be fully closed.

These two outlets are fitted with finger operated direction controls on the facia panel. Fully rotating the right-hand knob clockwise and the left-hand knob anti-clockwise will cut off supply of air to the interior completely. Reverse rotation of the knobs will progressively re-direct the air-flow from the feet to the car interior.

Fan Switch

The heater fan (C, Fig. 35) for the car heating and ventilating system considerably increases the flow of air through the system and is controlled by a three position switch (marked "Fan").

Press the switch rocker to the central position for slow speed and to the lower position for maximum speed, whichever is required.

Operation of the fan is required mainly when the car is stationary or running at a slow speed. At higher road speeds it will be found possible to dispense with the fan as air will be forced through the system due to the passage of the car through the air.

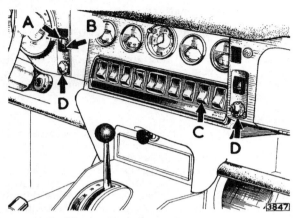

Fig. 35. Heating and ventilating controls.
A—Heater air control.
B—Heater temperature control.
C—Heater fan switch.
D—Heater outlet controls.

Cold Weather

To obtain fresh air heating, demisting and defrosting:
(a) Set fresh air control to DESIRED POSITION.
(b) Set temperature control to DESIRED POSITION.
(c) Switch ON fan at required speed.
(d) Open outlets.

To obtain rapid demisting and defrosting:
(a) Turn fresh air control to "FULLY ON".
(b) Set temperature control to "HOT".
(c) Switch ON fan—"FAST" position.
(d) Close outlets.

Warning—There is the possibility that fumes may be drawn into the car from the atmosphere when travelling in dense traffic and in such conditions it is advisable to close the heater air control and switch off the fan.

Hot Weather

To obtain ventilation and demisting:
(a) Set fresh air control to DESIRED POSITION.
(b) Set temperature control to "COLD".
(c) Switch ON fan at required speed.
(d) Open outlets (D, Fig. 35).

To obtain rapid demisting:
(a) Set fresh air control to "FULLY ON".
(b) Set temperature to "COLD".
(c) Switch ON fan—"FAST" position.
(d) Close outlets (D, Fig. 35).

AIR CONDITIONING SYSTEM (IF FITTED)

Operating Instructions

Car interior comfort may be controlled by the air volume (blower speed) switch "A" and the air temperature switch "B" (Fig. 36). Turning switch "A" from the OFF position starts the air flow from the supply outlet and also engages the compressor clutch. The switch has three blower speed positions: LOW—MEDIUM—HIGH.

Turning switch "B" clockwise increases the length of time that the compressor (and therefore refrigeration) stays on. The furthest position clockwise results in the coldest air.

To start the air conditioner, turn switch "B" to the required temperature setting. Turn switch "A" to select the required blower speed. Adjust the outlets to the desired position.

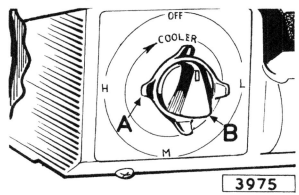

Fig. 36.   A—Air volume.   B—Air temperature.

To stop the air conditioner, turn switch "A" to the OFF position. This will switch off the blower and disengage the compressor clutch.

IMPORTANT: THE UNIT MUST ALWAYS BE SWITCHED OFF AFTER STOPPING THE ENGINE.

Operating Hints

If the air volume appears to decrease it is likely that the coil in the evaporator is freezing up. To correct, turn switch "B" counter-clockwise until the condition improves.

If the car interior becomes too cold even after setting the air volume on LOW, turn switch "B" counter-clockwise until the desired temperature is reached.

The air conditioner may be used to demist the **interior** of the windows during any weather conditions.

It is recommended that the air conditioner is operated for approximately 10-15 minutes per week during the winter (or cool) season. This will help to maintain the components of the system, particularly the compressor, in good working condition.

Note: A sight glass to indicate refrigerant level in the system is attached to the receiver/drier unit at the L.H. side of the engine compartment. If bubbles or foam appear while the compressor is running, the unit requires servicing by an Authorised Dealer.

The oil level in the compressor should be checked every 12 months (or before operating the air conditioning system following the winter season).

THIS SERVICE CAN ONLY BE CARRIED OUT BY AN AUTHORISED DEALER.

WINDSCREEN WASHING EQUIPMENT

The windscreen washer is electrically operated and comprises a plastic water container mounted in the engine compartment which is connected to jets at the base of the windscreen. Water is delivered to the jets by an electrically driven pump incorporated in the water container.

Operation

The windscreen washer should be used in conjunction with the windscreen wipers to remove foreign matter that settles on the windscreen.

Press the switch (marked "Washer") when the washer should operate immediately; release the switch when sufficient water has been delivered to the windscreen.

Warning—if the washer does not function immediately check that there is water in the container. The motor will be damaged if the switch is held pressed for more than one or two seconds if the water in the container is frozen.

The washer should not be used under freezing conditions as the fine jets of water spread over the windscreen by the blades will tend to freeze up.

In the summer the washer should be used freely to remove insects before they dry and harden on the screen.

Lucas "Crystal Clear" Screenjet fluid may be added to the water to assist removal and to dissolve greasy smears from the glass.

Filling-up

The water should be absolutely CLEAN. If possible, use SOFT water for filling the container, but if this is not obtainable and hard water has to be used, frequent operation and occasional attention to the nozzle outlet holes will be amply repaid in preventing the formation of unwelcome deposits.

The correct water level is up to the bottom of the container neck. Do not overfill, or unneccessary splashing may result. Always replace the filler cover correctly after filling.

It is not possible to empty the container completely with the pump. Refilling is necessary when the water level has fallen below the level of the pump.

Do not continue to operate the switch after the available water has been used up otherwise damage may be caused to the unit.

Refilling the container will restore normal operation of the unit.

Keep the pump filter clean and the container free from sediment.

Cold Weather

The Lucas 5 S J windscreen washer container which is made of high density polythene can be given a safe degree of protection from frost damage down to –28 deg. F. (–33 deg. C.) by the use of proprietary anti-freeze solvents as marketed by "TRICO" or "HOLTS".

Instruction regarding the solvent will be found on the container.

Denatured alcohol (Methylated Spirits) must NOT be used.
The use of this chemical will discolour the paintwork.

Adjusting the Jets

With the screwdriver turn the jet nozzle in the jet holder until the jets of water strike the windscreen in the area swept by the wiper blades. It may be

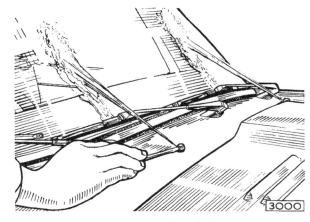

Fig. 38.   Adjusting the jets.

necessary to adjust the nozzle slightly after a trial on the road due to jets of water being deflected by the airstream.
On 2 + 2 cars, twin nozzles are incorporated in a single holder located rear centre of the bonnet.

Cleaning the Jet Nozzles

To clear a blocked jet nozzle completely unscrew the nozzle from the jet holder. Clear the small orifice with a piece of thin wire or blow out with compressed air; operate the washer with the nozzle removed. Allow the water to flush through the jet holder and then replace the nozzle.

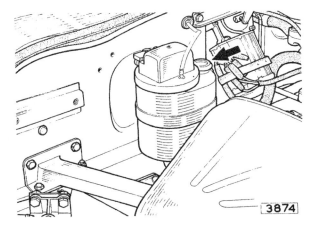

Fig. 37.   The windscreen washer container is replenished through a hole in the cap.

45

LOWERING AND RAISING THE HOOD
(Open 2-seater)

To Lower the Hood

1. Release the three fasteners retaining the hood to the windscreen surround by pulling down (Fig. 39).

2. Release the two hood rear retaining fasteners located inside the body at the rear of the doors (Fig. 40).

3. Lift the front of the hood and fold rearwards, *having first tilted the seats forward.*

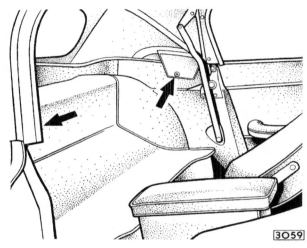

Fig. 40.

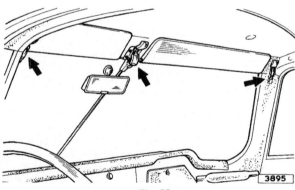

Fig. 39.

4. Fold under the plastic rear window taking care that the window is lying flat without any creases in the material. Complete the folding of the hood, pull the top of the hood material rearwards and fold in the corners. Ensure that the hood material is not trapped in the hood mechanism (Fig. 41).

46

5.   Collapse the frame and stow away at the rear of the seats.

6.   Pivot the two fastener straps secured to the header panel through 90 deg., pass the straps through the two holes in the header panel and fasten to the two outer snap fastener studs on the back panel (Fig. 42).

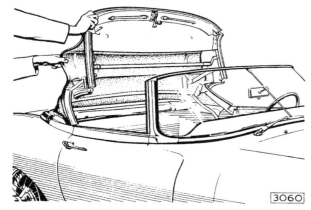

Fig. 41.

7.   To fit the cover, place over the folded hood, pull down and fasten the three straps to the three fastener studs on the back panel. Snap the two side fasteners to the fastener studs located inside the body at the rear of the doors (Fig. 43). Pull the cover rearwards and clip the four hooks under the chromium beading strip (located at the rear of the hood) (Fig. 44).

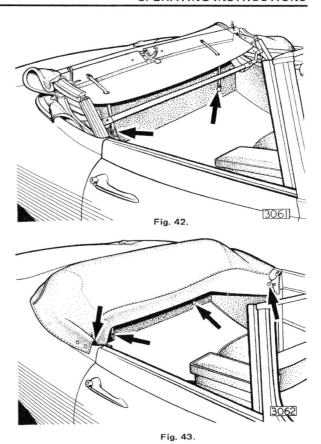

Fig. 42.

Fig. 43.

47

To Raise the Hood

1. Release the three straps, the two side snap fasteners and the four hook fasteners retaining the hood cover in position. Remove cover. Tilt seats forward.
2. Raise the hood and pull up to the windscreen surround.
3. Engage the catch hooks and pull up the levers.
4. Snap on the two fasteners located inside the body at the rear of the doors.

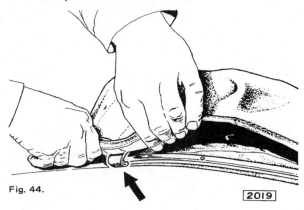

Fig. 44.   2019

DETACHABLE HARDTOP

To Remove the Hardtop:

1. Release the three fasteners retaining the hardtop to the windscreen surround by pulling down the levers.

2. Lower the windows.
3. Remove the two retaining bolts and lift off (Fig. 45).

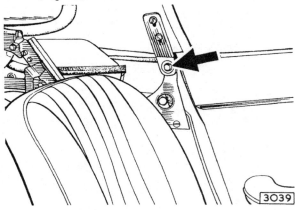

Fig. 45.   Hardtop retaining bolts.

Fig. 46.   The battery indicator.

BATTERY INDICATOR

Check the condition of the battery by means of the panel shown below.

RED (Off Charge)		NORMAL			RED (On Charge)
BATTERY CHARGE EXTREMELY LOW	BATTERY CHARGE LOW	WELL CHARGED BATTERY	CHARGING VOLTAGE LOW	CHARGING VOLTAGE SATISFACTORY	CHARGING VOLTAGE TOO HIGH
If with the ignition and electrical equipment e.g. headlamps etc., switched on, but with the engine not running the indicator settles in this section—your battery requires attention.		Ideally the indicator should settle in this section when the ignition and electrical equipment e.g. headlamps etc., are switched on and the engine is not running.	This condition may be indicated when the headlights and other equipment are in use.	The indicator should point to this section when the engine is running above idle.	If the indicator continues to point to this section after 10 minutes running, either your voltage regulator requires adjustment or some other fault has developed.

IMPORTANT   All readings on the indicator should be ignored when the engine is idling, since readings may vary at very slow engine speeds due solely to operation of the voltage regulator.

OFF CHARGE

This means more energy is being used from your battery than is being replaced by the alternator on your car. This condition is satisfactory provided it does not persist for long periods, when the engine is running above idle or at speed. If the indicator remains in the section, it may mean that you have a broken or slipping fan belt, a faulty alternator, a badly adjusted voltage regulator or some other fault.

ON CHARGE

This means your battery is having more energy put into it than is being taken out of it. In the ordinary way this condition predominates and your battery is continuously being recharged by the alternator whenever the engine is running above idle. If however the engine is continually running slowly as may be the case in traffic—or when, in winter, lights and cold starting make extra demands on the battery—you may find the rate of discharge exceeds the rate of charge—that is to say the battery is running down, as will be indicated on your Battery Condition Indicator and you may need an extra charge if 'battery charge low or extremely low" is indicated by the instrument.

IMPORTANT

MAINTENANCE

When you take delivery of your new car you will do so with the knowledge that your Dealer has completed a pre-delivery check to ensure that the vehicle is in first class condition.

To keep the car in this condition it is necessary for certain small items to receive regular attention from the owner between the periods of normal servicing. It is strongly recommended that **EACH DAY the levels of Engine Oil and Radiator Coolant** are checked and topped up as necessary.
EACH WEEK your Filling Station attendant should be requested to **examine the water level in the Battery and Screen Washer Bottle and check tyre pressures.**

It is normally recommended that the engine sump should be drained and refilled with new oil at 6,000 miles (10,000 Km.) periods. If the car is regularly used for short journeys or if heavy traffic conditions predominate, it is earnestly suggested that engine oil should be changed every 3,000 miles (5,000 Km.).

50

BRAKE SERVO

The brakes of this car are assisted in operation by a Vacuum Servo which will only operate when the engine is running.

Increased pressure on the brake pedal is required to operate the brakes when the servo is not in action.

Do not coast the car in neutral with the engine switched off.

BRAKES

To obtain satisfactory braking from high speeds your car is fitted with brake friction pads which are manufactured of a hard material having a relatively low coefficient of friction.

To obtain fully satisfactory results it is important that careful attention is paid to the following points during the first 1,000 miles running of your car.

1. Other than in the case of emergency, avoid heavy braking. (Heavy braking or rough usage of the brakes before the friction pads are fully bedded can result in damage being caused to the friction pads and brake discs).

2. Frequent light application of the brakes is desirable to obtain full bedding of the brake friction pads before the normal running-in period is completed and the car operated at high speeds, when maximum brake efficiency will be required.

ROUTINE MAINTENANCE

FUEL REQUIREMENTS FOR 9 TO 1 and 8 TO 1
COMPRESSION RATIO ENGINES

If the engine of your car is fitted with 9 to 1 compression ratio pistons (indicated by 9 after the engine number) use only Super grade fuel with a minimum octane rating of 98. (Research method.) If a car is fitted with 8 to 1 compression ratio pistons (indicated by 8 after the engine number) use Premium grade fuel with a minimum rating of 94. (Research method.).

In the United Kingdom use '5 STAR' (9: 1) or '4 STAR' (8: 1) petrol.

If, of necessity, the car has to be operated on lower octane fuel do not use full throttle otherwise detonation may occur with resultant piston trouble.

1,000 MILES (1600 KM)

FREE SERVICE

1. Road test and check for oil, petrol, hydraulic fluid or coolant leaks.
2. Check torque loading of cylinder head nuts.
3. Check oil or fluid levels and top up as necessary :—
   - (a) Brake reservoirs,
   - (b) Clutch reservoir (if fitted),
   - (c) Power steering reservoir (if fitted),
   - (d) Top up carburetter hydraulic dampers and check carburation,
   - (e) Battery,
   - (f) Screen washer bottle,
   - (g) Radiator header tank (add anti-freeze when necessary),
   - (h) Manual gearbox,
   - (i) Final drive unit.
4. Drain and refill
   - (a) Engine sump,
   - (b) Automatic transmission unit (if fitted).
5. Adjust front band on automatic transmission unit (if fitted).
6. Check driving belts for correct tension.
7. Clean and adjust contact-breaker points.
8. Check all brake pipe unions, petrol pipe unions, and hoses for leakage.
9. Check tightness of all front and rear suspension bolts and nuts.
10. Check tightness of nuts on all steering connections including column universal joints.
11. Check tightness of road wheel nuts and wheel alignment.
12. Check tyres for damage and adjust pressures.
13. Check operation of all lights and systems.
14. Check door locks and bonnet release control.
15. Lubricate all grease nipples (excluding wheel bearings).

3,000 MILES (5,000 KM)

CHECK SERVICE

Repeat these servicing items at the under-mentioned subsequent periods :—

9,000 miles	(15,000 Km.)
15,000 miles	(25,000 Km.)
21,000 miles	(35,000 Km.)
27,000 miles	(45,000 Km.)
33,000 miles	(55,000 Km.)
39,000 miles	(65,000 Km.)
45,000 miles	(75,000 Km.)
51,000 miles	(85,000 Km.)
57,000 miles	(95,000 Km.)
63,000 miles	(105,000 Km.)
69,000 miles	(115,000 Km.)

1. Check oil or fluid levels and top up as necessary :—
   - (a) Engine sump,
   - (b) Brake reservoirs,
   - (c) Clutch reservoir (if fitted),
   - (d) Power steering reservoir (if fitted),
   - (e) Top up carburetter hydraulic dampers and check carburation,
   - (f) Battery,
   - (g) Screen washer bottle,
   - (h) Radiator header tank (add anti-freeze when necessary),
   - (i) Manual gearbox,
   - (j) Final drive unit.
2. Check driving belts for correct tension.
3. Examine brake pads for wear and check operation of brake stop lights.
4. Examine tyres for damage and adjust pressures.
5. Check tightness of road wheel nuts.

6,000 MILES (10,000 KM)

MINOR SERVICE

Repeat these servicing items at the under-mentioned subsequent periods : —

18,000 miles	(30,000 Km.)
30,000 miles	(50,000 Km.)
42,000 miles	(70,000 Km.)
54,000 miles	(90,000 Km.)
66,000 miles	(110,000 Km.)

1. Check oil or fluid levels and top up as necessary :-
    - (a)   Brake reservoirs,
    - (b)   Clutch reservoir (if fitted),
    - (c)   Power steering reservoir (if fitted),
    - (d)   Top up carburetter dampers,
    - (e)   Battery and check connections,
    - (f)   Screen washer bottle,
    - (g)   Radiator header tank (add anti-freeze when necessary),
    - (h)   Manual gearbox or automatic transmission unit,
    - (i)   Final drive unit.
2. Drain and refill : —
    - (a)   Engine sump. Fit new oil filter element and seal.
3. Check driving belts for correct tension.
4. Check brake pads for wear and advise wear-rate to owner.
5. Check tyres for damage and tread depth. If uneven wear evident, check wheel alignment. Adjust pressures.
6. Check tightness of road wheel nuts.
7. Check headlamp alignment and functioning of mandatory lights including stop lights.
8. Lubricate all grease nipples, excluding wheel bearings.
9. Renew fuel filter element and seals.

12,000 MILES (20,000 KM)

MAJOR SERVICE

Repeat these servicing items at the under-mentioned subsequent periods :—

24,000 miles (40,000 Km.)
48,000 miles (80,000 Km.)
60,000 miles (100,000 Km.)

1. Check oil or fluid levels and top up as necessary :—
   - (a) Brake reservoirs,
   - (b) Clutch reservoir (if fitted),
   - (c) Power steering reservoir (if fitted),
   - (d) Top up carburetter hydraulic dampers,
   - (e) Battery and check connections,
   - (f) Screen washer bottle,
   - (g) Radiator header tank (add anti-freeze when necessary),
   - (h) Automatic transmission,
   - (i) Final drive unit.
2. Drain and refill :—
   - (a) Engine sump. Fit new oil filter element and seal,
   - (b) Manual gearbox. Clean overdrive filter (if fitted),
   - (c) Final drive unit (if 'Powr-Lok' differential fitted. Use only special limited slip oil).
3. Renew sparking plugs.
4. Renew air cleaner element and fuel line filter element.
5. Clean and adjust contact breaker points. Check operation of centrifugal advance mechanism. Lubricate distributor.
6. Check driving belts for wear and tension.
7. Adjust top timing chain if required.
8. Lubricate all grease nipples including front and rear wheel bearings.
9. Check all suspension and exhaust mountings for security.
10. Check all steering connections, ball joints etc., for security and wear.

12,000 Miles (20,000 Km)
—continued

Repeat these servicing items at the under-mentioned subsequent periods: —

24,000 miles (40,000 Km.)
48,000 miles (80,000 Km.)
60,000 miles (100,000 Km.)

11. Check brake pads for degree of wear and advise wear-rate to owner.
12. Check functioning of all mandatory lights including stop lights and alignment of headlamps.
13. Check tyres for damage and tread depth. If uneven wear evident, check wheel alignment. Adjust pressures.
14. Oil can lubrication of door locks, bonnet hinges and locks, boot hinges and lock, seat slides, fuel filler flap hinges, control linkages.
15. Detect and report any oil, petrol, water, hydraulic fluid leakage and damaged hoses or other damaged parts.

24,000 Miles (40,000Km)
ADDITIONAL SERVICE

1. Brake system. Drain off old fluid, retract pistons in brake calipers to complete operation. Flush out system, and refill with new fluid.

48,000 Miles (80,000 Km)
ADDITIONAL SERVICE

1. Overhaul complete brake system.

36,000 MILES (60,000 KM)

MAJOR SERVICE

Repeat these servicing items at the under-mentioned subsequent period :—

72,000 miles (120,000 Km.)

1. Check oil or fluid levels and top up as necessary :—
    - (a)   Clutch reservoir (if fitted),
    - (b)   Power steering reservoir (if fitted),
    - (c)   Top up carburetter hydraulic dampers,
    - (d)   Battery and check connections,
    - (e)   Screen washer bottle,
    - (f)   Radiator header tank (add anti-freeze when necessary),
    - (g)   Automatic transmission,
    - (h)   Final drive unit.
2. Drain and refill
    - (a)   Engine sump. Fit new oil filter element and seal,
    - (b)   Manual gearbox. Clean overdrive filter (if fitted),
    - (c)   Final drive unit (if 'Powr-Lok' differential fitted. Use only special limited slip oil).
3. Renew sparking plugs.
4. Renew air cleaner element and fuel line filter element.
5. Clean and adjust contact breaker points. Check operation of centrifugal advance mechanism. Lubricate distributor.
6. Check driving belts for wear and tension.
7. Adjust top timing chain if required.
8. Lubricate all grease nipples including front and rear wheel bearings.
9. Check all suspension and exhaust mounting for security.
10. Check all steering connections, ball joints etc., for security and wear.

36,000 Miles (60,000 Km)
—continued

Repeat these servicing items at the under-mentioned subsequent period:—

72,000 miles (120,000 Km.)

11. Check brake pads for degree of wear and advise wear-rate to owner.
12. Check functioning of all mandatory lights including stop lights and alignment of headlamps.
13. Check tyres for damage and tread depth. If uneven wear evident, check wheel alignment. Adjust pressures.
14. Oil can lubrication of door locks, bonnet hinges and lock, boot hinges, and lock, seat slides, fuel filler flap hinges, control linkages.
15. Detect and report any oil, petrol, water, hydraulic fluid leakage and damaged hoses or other damaged parts.

RECOMMENDED LUBRICANTS

Component	MOBIL	CASTROL	SHELL	ESSO	B.P.	DUCKHAM	TEXACO
Engine	Mobil Super or Mobil Special	Castrol GTX	Shell Super Oil	Uniflow	Super Visco-Static 10W/40	Q20–50 or Q5500	Havoline 20W/40 or 10W/30
Upper cylinder lubrication	Mobil Upperlube	Castrollo	Shell U.C.L. or Donax U.	Esso U.C.L.	U.C.L.	Adcoid Liquid	Texaco U.C.L.
Distributor oil can points Oil can lubrication	Mobiloil A	Castrol GTX	Shell Super Oil	Uniflow	Energol SAE 30	Q20–50	Havoline 30
Gearbox Final Drive Unit (not 'Powr-Lok')	Mobilube GX 90	Castrol Hypoy	Spirax 90 E P	Esso Gear Oil GX 90/140	Gear Oil SAE 90 E P	Hypoid 90	Multigear Lubricant EP.90
Front wheel bearings Rear wheel bearings Distributor cam Final drive half-shafts Steering tie-rods Wheel swivels Door hinges Steering housing	Mobil-grease MP	Castrolease LM	Retinax A	Esso Multi-purpose Grease H	Energrease L.2	LB 10	Marfak All Purpose
Automatic transmission unit Power steering system	ATF.201	Castrol T.Q.F.	Shell Donax T7	Esso Glide	BP Autran B	Q-matic	Texamatic 6691

SERVICE INSTRUCTIONS

RECOMMENDED HYDRAULIC FLUID

Braking System and Clutch Operation

Castrol/Girling Crimson Clutch/Brake Fluid is recommended. This conforms to S.A.E. J1703A specification modified for additional safety to give a higher boiling point.

Where this is not available, only fluid guaranteed to conform to S.A.E. J1703A specification may be used as an alternative after fully draining and flushing the system.

IMPORTANT

If the car is fitted with Stromberg carburetters (U.S.A. and Canada only) consult your Jaguar Distributor or Dealer for all details of carburetter tuning and ignition timing. Tuning by unqualified persons or personnel must NOT be attempted.

ENGINE

Checking the Engine Oil Level

Check the oil level with the car standing on level ground otherwise a false reading will be obtained.

Remove the dipstick and wipe it dry. Replace and withdraw the dipstick; if the oil level is on the knurled patch, with the engine hot or cold, no additional oil is required. **If the engine has been run immediately prior to making an oil level check, wait one minute after switching off before checking the oil level.**

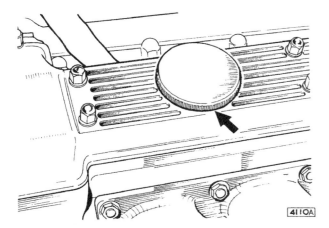

Fig. 47.   Engine oil filler.

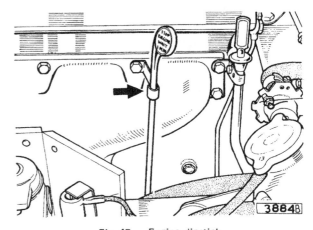

Fig. 48.   Engine dipstick.

Changing the Engine Oil

The draining of the sump should be carried out at the end of a run when the oil is hot and therefore will flow more freely. The drain plug is situated at the right-hand rear corner of the sump.

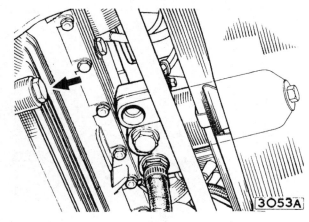

Fig. 49.   Engine drain plug.

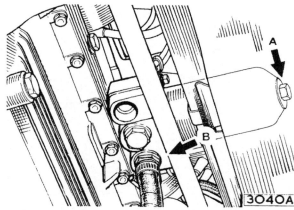

Fig. 50.   Engine oil filter
A—securing bolt.
B—Oil pressure relief valve union.

Oil Filter Element

To guard against the possibility of the filter being neglected to the extent where the element becomes completely choked, a balance valve is incorporated in the filter head which allows **unfiltered** oil to by-pass the element and reach the bearings. This will be accompanied by a drop in normal oil pressure of some 10 lb. per sq. in. and, if this occurs, the filter element **must** be changed as soon as possible.

To gain access to the filter, remove the drive screw retaining the filter cover plate to the R.H. undershield and withdraw the cover. Unscrew the central bolt and remove the canister and element. Thoroughly wash the canister in petrol and allow to dry out.

When re-assembling with a new element in place, renew the circular rubber seal in the filter head.

Water Pump Drive Belt

The drive belt should be examined for wear periodically. Routine adjustment is not necessary as the belt is automatically adjusted by means of a spring loaded jockey pulley.

Alternator Drive Belt

The drive belt should be examined for wear and correct tension at the recommended periods.

To increase the belt tension, release the bolts A, B, C, (Fig. 51) and swing the alternator away from the engine until it is possible to depress the belt 1/2" (12 mm) midway between the two pulleys.

To remove the belt, swing the alternator towards the engine.

Note: If the car is fitted with the Air Conditioning Equipment the alternator will be mounted between the cam shaft covers. The adjustment details remain basically the same as detailed above.

Top Timing Chain Tension

If the top timing chain is audible adjust the tension as follows:—

This operation requires the use of a special tool to enable the adjuster plate to be rotated. To gain access to the adjuster plate remove the breather housing attached to the front face of the cylinder head.

Slacken the locknut securing the serrated adjuster plate. Tension the chain by pressing the locking plunger inwards and rotating the adjuster plate in an anti-clockwise direction.

When correctly tensioned there should be slight flexibility on both sides of the chain below the camshaft sprockets, that is, the chain must not be dead tight. Release locking plunger, and securely tighten locknut. Refit the breather housing.

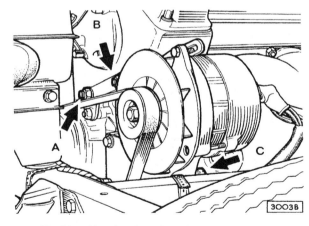

Fig. 51. Showing the alternator mounting bolts.

Distributor—Lubrication (Fig. 52)

Take care to prevent oil or grease from getting on or near the contact breaker points.

Remove the moulded cap at the top of the distributor by springing back the two clips. Lift off the rotor arm and apply a few drops of engine oil around the screw (4) now exposed. It is not necessary to remove the screw as it has clearance to permit the passage of oil. Apply **one** drop of oil to the post (1) on which the contact breaker pivots. Lightly smear the cam (3) with grease. Lubricate the centrifugal advance mechanism by injecting a few drops of engine oil

through the aperture at the edge of the contact breaker base plate (2).

Distributor Contact Breaker Points (Fig. 53)

Check the gap between the contact points with feeler gauges when the points are fully opened by one of the cams on the distributor shaft. A combined

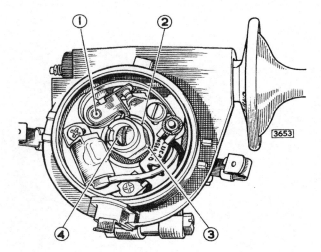

Fig. 52.   Distributor lubrication points.

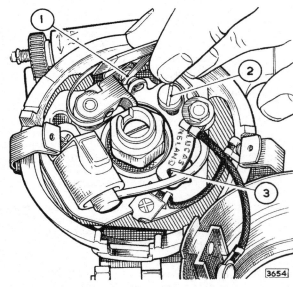

Fig. 53.   Checking the gap between the distributor contact points (1). The screw (2) secures the fixed contact plate; the gap is adjusted by turning a screwdriver in the slot (3) in the contact plate.

screwdriver and feeler gauge is provided in the tool kit.

The correct gap is 0.014 in.–0.016 in. (0.36 mm.–0.41 mm.).

If the gap is incorrect, slacken (very slightly) the contact plate securing screw and adjust the gap by turning a screwdriver in the nick in the contact plate and the slot in the base plate, clockwise to decrease the gap and anti-clockwise to increase the gap. Tighten the securing screw and recheck the gap.

Examine the contact breaker points. If the contacts are burned or blackened, clean them with a fine carborundum stone or very fine emery cloth.

Afterwards wipe away any trace of grease or metal dust with a petrol moistened cloth.

Cleaning of the contacts is made easier if the contact breaker lever carrying the moving contact is removed. To do this, remove the nut, insulating piece and connections from the post to which the end of the contact breaker spring is anchored. The contact breaker lever can now be lifted off its pivot post.

Check Ignition Timing

Set the micrometer adjustment in the centre of the scale.

Rotate the engine until the rotor arm approaches the No. 6 (front) cylinder segment in the distributor cap.

Slowly rotate the engine until the ignition timing scale on the crankshaft damper is the appropriate number of degrees (see "Data") before the pointer on the lower left-hand side of the timing chain cover.

Connect a 12 volt test lamp with one lead to the distributor terminal (or the CB terminal of the ignition coil) and the other to a good earth.

Slacken the distributor clamping plate pinch bolt.

Switch on the ignition.

Slowly rotate the distributor body until the points are just breaking, that is, when the lamp lights up.

Tighten the distributor plate pinch bolt.

A maximum of six clicks on the vernier adjustment from this setting to either advance or retard, is allowed.

Check the centrifugal advance mechanism of the distributor with a stroboscopic timing light having first disconnected the vacuum advance unit.

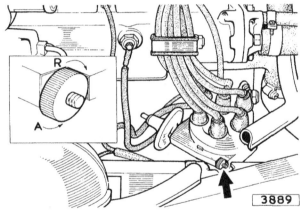

Fig. 54.   Distributor advance and retard mechanism.

Sparking Plugs

The only efficient way to clean sparking plugs is to have them properly serviced on machines specially designed for this purpose.

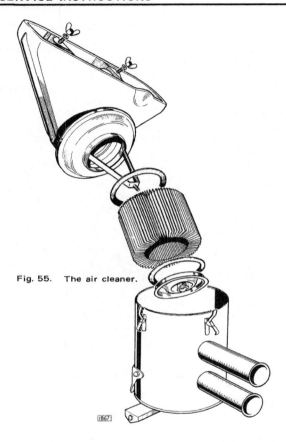

Fig. 55.   The air cleaner.

The gap between the points should be 0.025 in. (0.64 mm.). When adjusting the gap always move the side wire— never bend the centre wire.

Air Cleaner

The air cleaner is of the paper element type and is situated in the engine compartment on the right-hand side adjacent to the carburetters.

To gain access to the element release the three spring clips retaining top cover to base. Remove two wing nuts attaching cleaner to air box and lift out element and cover. Remove serrated nut, and retainer plate from base of unit and withdraw element.

Crankcase Breather

Disconnect the breather pipe from the housing at the front of the cylinder head.

Remove the nuts securing the housing and withdraw the flametrap.

Wash the flametrap thoroughly in petrol and replace.

Renew the gaskets on each side of the flametrap.

Reconnect the breather pipe and check that all clamps are tight allowing no air leaks.

Fig. 56.   The crankcase breather.

CARBURETTERS AND FUEL SYSTEM

Lubricate Carburetter Piston Damper
Each carburetter is fitted with a hydraulic piston damper which unless periodically replenished with oil, will cause poor acceleration and spitting back through the carburetter on rapid opening of the throttle.

To replenish with oil, unscrew the cap on top of suction chambers and lift out the damper valve which is attached to the cap. Fill the hollow piston spindle, which can be seen down inside the bore of the suction chamber, with SAE 20 engine oil.

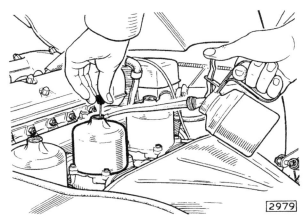

2979

Fig. 57.   Topping up the hydraulic piston damper.

Checking Carburetter Slow Running
(a)   Cars fitted with synchromesh gearbox
The idling speed of the engine when fully warmed up should be set at 700 r.p.m.

Note: If the idling speed is less than 700 r.p.m. or if the engine is not idling smoothly, chatter from the constant mesh gears may be noticeable.

(b)   Cars fitted with automatic transmission (2 + 2)
The idling speed of the engine when fully warmed up should be set at 600 r.p.m. with P or N selected—there will be a slight reduction of idling speed when D1 or D2 is engaged.

If adjustment is required turn the three slow running volume screws (see Fig. 60) **by exactly equal amounts** until the idling speed observed on the revolution counter instrument, is correct.

Cleaning Carburetter Filters
(S.U. carburetters only)
Removal of the bolt securing the petrol pipe banjo union to each float chamber will expose the filters. Remove the filters and clean in petrol; do not use a cloth as particles will stick to the gauze.

When refitting, insert the filter with the spring first and ensure that the fibre washers are replaced one to each side of the banjo union.

67

Fuel Feed Line Filter Bowl

The filter bowl is attached to the bulkhead (right-hand side) and is of the glass bowl type with a renewable filter element.

To renew the element, slacken the locking nut; swing the retaining clip to one side and remove the bowl, sealing washers and element. Discard the element. Wash the bowl thoroughly in petrol.

Fit a new element with sealing washers and re-assemble the unit.

Note: If the sediment build-up is obviously excessive, the filter should be renewed more frequently than is recommended.

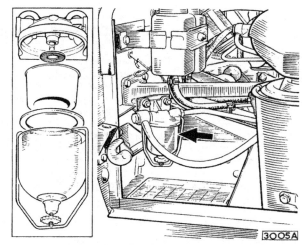

Fig. 59.   Fuel feed line filter.

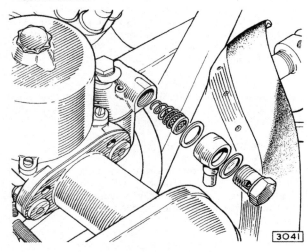

Fig. 58.   Carburetter filter removal.

Tuning

It is useless to attempt carburetter tuning until the cylinder compressions, valve clearances, sparking plug gaps and contact breaker point gaps have been tested, checked and adjusted, if necessary. The distributor centrifugal advance mechanism and vacuum advance operation should be checked and ignition timing set to the figure given under "General Data", with the centrifugal advance and vacuum advance mechanisms in the static position. For final road test, adjustment of not more than six clicks of the micrometer adjustment at the distributor to either advance or retard is permitted. The ignition setting is important since if retarded or advanced too far the setting of the carburetters will be affected. As the needle size is determined during engine development, tuning of the carburetters is confined to the correct idling setting. The air intake should be removed and the engine run until it has attained its normal operating temperature. Release the three pinch bolts securing the two piece throttle levers to the carburetter throttle spindles.

butterfly valve fully by rotating the throttle spindle in a clockwise direction looking from the front; with the throttle held closed tighten the pinch bolt keeping the two piece throttle lever in the midway position.

Repeat for the other two carburetters, then operate the accelerator linkage and observe if all the throttles are opening simultaneously by noting the movement of the full throttle stops at the left-hand side of the throttle spindles.

Note: On initial movement of the accelerator linkage there should be a limited amount of lost motion at the throttle spindles; this ensures that all the throttle butterfly valves can return to the fully closed position.

Screw down the slow running volume screws (A, Fig. 60) on to their seatings and then unscrew 2 full turns. Remove the piston and suction chambers; disconnect the jet control linkage by removing the clevis pins from the connecting rod fork ends underneath the front and rear carburetters. Unscrew the mixture adjusting screws (C) until each jet is flush with the bridge of its carburetter. Replace the pistons and suction chambers and check that each piston falls freely on to the bridge of its carburetter (by means of

the piston lifting pin). Turn down the mixture adjusting screws 2½ turns.

Restart the engine and adjust to the desired idling speed of 700 r.p.m. (600 r.p.m. automatic transmission) by moving each slow running volume screw an equal amount. By listening to the hiss in the intakes, adjust the slow running screws until the intensity of the hiss is similar on all intakes. This will synchronise the mixture flow of the three carburetters.

When this is satisfactory the mixture should be adjusted by screwing all the mixture adjusting screws up (weaker) or down (richer) by the same amount until the fastest idling speed is obtained consistant with even firing.

As the mixture is adjusted, the engine will probably run faster and it may therefore be necessary to screw down the slow running volume screws in order to reduce the speed.

Now check the mixture strength by lifting the piston of the front carburetter by approximately 1/32 in. (0.8 mm.) when, if:

(a)   the engine speed increases and **continues to run faster,** this indicates that the mixture is too rich.

(b)   the engine speed immediately decreases, this indicates that the mixture is too weak.

(c)   the engine speed **momentarily** increases very slightly, this indicates that the mixture is correct.

Repeat the operation at the remaining two carburetters and after adjustment re-check the front carburetter since the carburetters are interdependent. When the mixture is correct, the exhaust note should be regular and even. If it is irregular with a splashy type of misfire and colourless exhaust, the mixture is too weak. If there is a regular or rhythmical type of misfire in the exhaust beat together with a blackish exhaust, then the mixture is too rich.

When reconnecting the jet operating cable allow 1/16 in. (1.5 mm.) free travel at the bottom of the facia panel control before the jet levers begin to move.

Fast Idle Setting

Pull out the choke lever on the facia panel to a point immediately short of the position where the mixture adjusting screw levers (C) begin to move. This will be approaching the mid-travel position of the control knob and approximates to 5/8 in. (16 mm.) movement at the bottom of the jet levers. Adjust the fast idle screws (B) on the throttle stops to give an engine speed of about 1,000 r.p.m. (when hot).

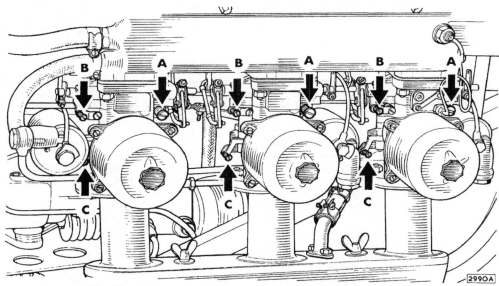

Fig. 60.   Carburetter tuning.

A—Slow running volume screw.
B—Fast idle screw.
C—Mixture adjusting screw.

COOLING SYSTEM

Checking Radiator Coolant Level

The cooling system is sealed and the level must be checked at the expansion tank and NOT at the radiator top tank.

Check when the system is COLD.

Remove the pressure cap and top up to the half-way mark in the tank.

When checking, care must be taken to ensure that the radiator and expansion tank caps are not reversed. The radiator top tank cap is **plain** and is **not** pressurised. The expansion tank cap is pressurised at 7 lb. per sq. in. (13 lb. per sq. in. on cars fitted with air conditioning).

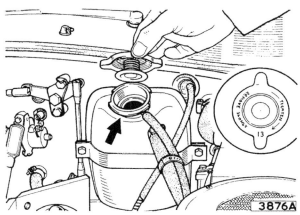

Fig. 61. Expansion tank filler cap. Inset shows cap when air conditioning is fitted.

Care of the Cooling System

The entire cooling system should occasionally be flushed out to remove sediment. To do this, open the radiator drain tap and remove cylinder block drain plug and insert a water hose into the radiator neck. Allow the water to flow through the system, with the engine running at a fast idle speed (1,000 r.p.m.) to cause circulation, until the water runs clear.

Since deposits in the water will in time cause fouling of the surfaces of the cooling system with consequent impaired efficiency it is desirable to retard this tendency as much as possible by using water as nearly neutral (soft) as is available. One of the approved brands of water inhibitor may be used with advantage

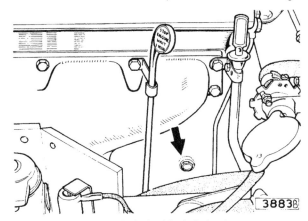

Fig. 62. Cylinder block drain plug.

71

to obviate the creation of deposits in the system.
Check the radiator water level after running the
engine and top up if necessary.

Refilling the Cooling System—Important
When refilling the cooling system following complete
drainage, place the heater temperature control in the
"Hot" position to allow the heater system to be filled
with coolant. Re-check the level after running the
engine for a short period.

Fig. 63.   Radiator drain tap.

3043

CLUTCH

Clutch Fluid Level Right-Hand Drive Cars
The fluid reservoir for the hydraulically operated clutch is situated on the bulkhead (adjacent to the brake reservoir), on the driver's side, and it is important that the fluid does not fall below the level marked "Fluid Level".

Left-Hand Drive Cars
The fluid reservoir for the hydraulically operated clutch is situated on the exhaust manifold adjacent to the twin brake reservoirs.

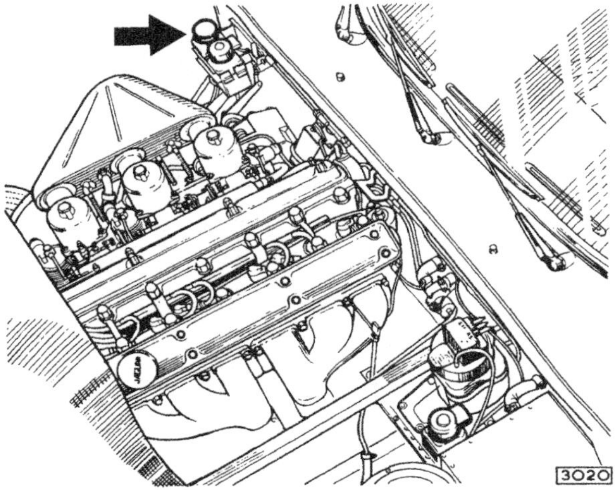

Fig. 64.   Clutch fluid reservoir—right-hand drive.

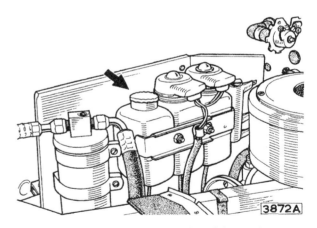

Fig. 65.   Clutch fluid reservoir—left-hand drive.

Bleeding the Clutch Hydraulic System

"Bleeding" the clutch hydraulic system (expelling the air) is not a routine maintenance operation and should only be necessary when a portion of the hydraulic system has been disconnected or if the level of the fluid in the reservoir has been allowed to fall. The presence of air in the hydraulic system may result in difficulty in engaging gear owing to the clutch not disengaging fully.

The procedure is as follows:—

Fill up the reservoir with brake fluid exercising great care to prevent the entry of dirt. Attach a rubber bleed tube to the nipple on the slave cylinder on the right-hand side of the clutch housing and allow the tube to hang in a clean glass jar partly filled with brake fluid. Unscrew the nipple one complete turn. Depress the clutch pedal slowly, tighten the bleeder nipple before the pedal reaches the end of its travel and allow the pedal to return unassisted.

Repeat the above procedure, closing the bleed nipple at each stroke, until the fluid issuing from the tube is entirely free of air, care being taken that the reservoir is replenished **frequently** during this operation, for should it be allowed to become empty more air will enter.

On completion, top up the reservoir to the bottom of the filler neck.

Do not on any account use the fluid which has been bled through the system to replenish the reservoir as it will have become aerated. Always use fresh fluid straight from the tin. Use only the recommended fluid.

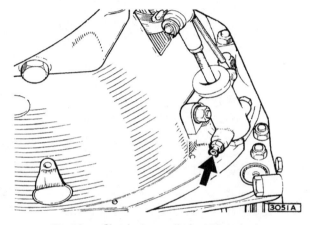

Fig. 66.   Clutch slave cylinder bleed nipple.

GEARBOX

Gearbox Oil Level

Check the level of the oil in the gearbox with the car standing on level ground.

A combined level and filler plug is fitted on the left-hand side of the gearbox. Clean off any dirt from around the plug before removing it.

The level of the oil should be to the bottom of the filler and level plug hole.

The filler plug is accessible from inside the car through aperture in the left-hand vertical face of the gearbox cowl. To obtain access to the plug, slide the seat rearwards to the full extent; lift the front carpet and roll forward to expose the two snap fasteners retaining the gearbox cowl covering to the floor.

Release the snap fasteners and raise the panel.

Remove the front aperture cover now exposed and insert a box spanner through the aperture to remove the plug.

In the interests of cleanliness always cover the carpets before carrying out lubrication.

Changing the Gearbox Oil

The draining of the gearbox should be carried out at the end of a run when the oil is hot and therefore will flow more freely. The drain plug is situated at the front end of the gearbox casing.

After all the oil has drained replace the drain plug and refill the gearbox with the recommended grade of oil through the combined filler and level plug hole situated on the left-hand side (early cars) right-hand side later cars of the gearbox casing; the level should be to the bottom of the hole.

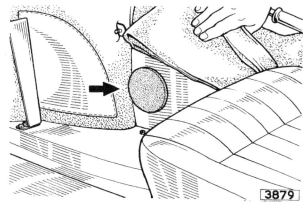

3879

Fig. 67.   Showing the location of the gearbox level and filler plug aperture in the side of the gearbox cowl.

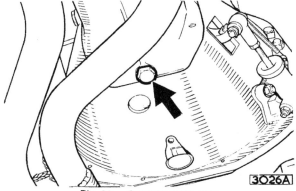

3026A

Fig. 68.   Gearbox drain plug.

AUTOMATIC TRANSMISSION (2 + 2)

Check Transmission Fluid Level

The transmission filler tube and dipstick are located on the left-hand side of the engine adjacent to the engine oil dipstick.

Before checking the fluid level, the car should be on level ground and the transmission should be at the normal operating temperature.

Set the handbrake and select P position.

The engine should be at normal idle.

While the engine is running, remove the dipstick, wipe clean and replace in the filler tube in its correct position.

Withdraw immediately and check.

If necessary, add fluid to bring the level to the "FULL" mark on the dipstick. The difference between "FULL" and "LOW" marks on the stick represents approximately 1½ pints (2 U.S. pints or 0.75 litres).

Be careful not to overfill.

If fluid is checked with the transmission cold, a false reading will be obtained and filling to the "FULL" mark will cause it to be overfilled.

If it is found necessary to add fluid frequently it will be an indication that there is a leakage in the transmission and it should be investigated immediately to prevent damage to the transmission.

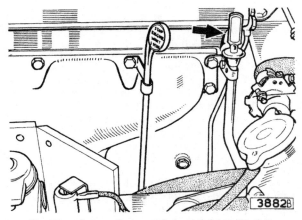

Fig. 69.   Automatic transmission oil filler dipstick.

FINAL DRIVE UNIT

Checking Final Drive Unit Oil Level
Check the level of the oil in the final drive unit with the car standing on level ground.
A combined filler and level plug is fitted in the rear of the differential casing accessible from underneath the car. Clean off any dirt from around the plug before removing it.
The level of the oil should be to the bottom of the filler and level plug hole; use only HYPOID oil of the correct grade and since different brands may not mix satisfactorily, draining and refilling is preferable to replenishing if the brand of the oil in the final drive is unknown.

Changing the Final Drive Unit Oil ('Powr-Lok' only)
The draining of the final drive should be carried out at the end of a run when the oil is hot and will therefore flow more freely. The drain plug is situated in the base of the differential casing.

After the oil has drained, replace the drain plug and refill the final drive unit with the recommended grade of oil after removal of the combined filler and level plug situated in rear cover.

The level of the oil should be at the bottom of the filler and level plug hole when the car is standing on level ground.

Use only HYPOID oil of the correct grade.

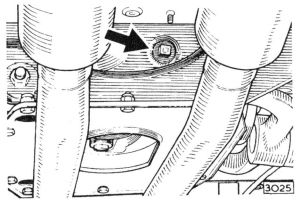

Fig. 70.   Final Drive Unit oil filler and level plug.

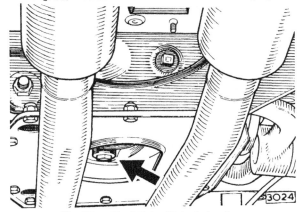

Fig. 71.   Final Drive Unit drain plug.

FRONT SUSPENSION AND STEERING

Front Shock Absorbers

The front shock absorbers are telescopic and contain no provision for replenishment of fluid.

Steering Housing

The steering gear is of the rack and pinion type and is attached to the front cross member of the frame assembly. A grease nipple for the lubrication of the rack and pinion housing is accessible from underneath the front of the car from the driver's side.

Do not over lubricate the steering housing to the extent where the rubber bellows at the end of the housing become distended. Check that the clips at the end of the bellows are fully tightened otherwise the grease will escape from the housing.

Steering Tie-rods

Lubricate the ball joints of the two steering tie-rods with the recommended lubricant. A bleed hole is provided in each ball joint; the hole is covered by a nylon washer which lifts under pressure and indicates when sufficient lubricant has been applied. When carrying out this operation examine the rubber seals at the bottom of the ball housing to see if they have become displaced or split. In this event they should be repositioned or replaced as any dirt or water that enters the joint will cause premature wear.

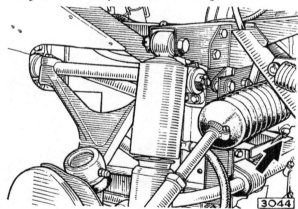

Fig. 72.   Steering housing grease nipple.

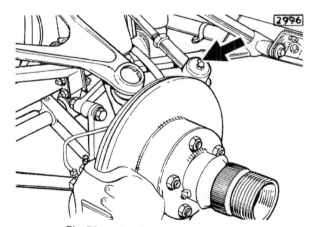

Fig. 73.   Steering tie rod grease nipple.

Wheel Swivels

Lubricate the nipples (four per car) fitted to the top and bottom of the wheel swivels.

A bleed hole is provided in each ball joint; the hole is covered by a nylon washer which lifts under pressure and indicates when sufficient lubricant has been applied.

The nipples are accessible from underneath the front of the car.

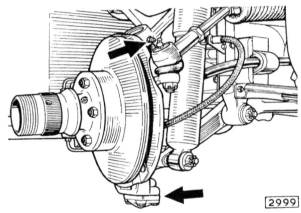

2999

Fig. 74.   Steering swivel grease nipples.

Front Wheel Alignment

As this operation requires the use of special tools it is best entrusted to a Jaguar dealer.

Front Wheel Camber Angle—Adjustment

Special links should be used when setting the camber angle of the front wheels. These links, which fit over the nuts securing the shock absorbers at top and bottom, hold the suspension in the mid-laden position. If the links are not available, additional weight should be added to the car to give a dimension of 13½ in. (34.29 cm.) between the centres of the shock absorber mountings which will be the mid-laden point of the front suspension.

Ensure that the tyre pressures are correct and that the car is standing on a level surface.

Camber Angle (¼ deg. $\pm$ ½ deg.) positive.

Note: The camber angle for each wheel must not vary by more than ½ deg.

Line up the front wheel being checked parallel to the centre line of the car. Using an approved gauge, check the camber angle. Rotate the wheel being checked through 180 deg. and re-check.

Adjustment is effected by removing or adding shims between the front suspension top wishbone bracket and the frame member.

When removing or adding shims note that the top holes in the shims are slotted and the bolts need only be slackened off; the bottom holes are not slotted and it is necessary therefore to remove the fixing bolts completely.

Inserting shims increases positive camber; removing shims increases negative camber or decreases positive camber. Remove or add an equal thickness of shims from each position, otherwise the castor angle will be affected. It should be noted that 1/16 in. (1.6 mm.) of shimming will alter the camber angle by approximately ¼ deg.

Check the other front wheel in a similar manner.
If any adjustment is made to the camber angle, the front wheel alignment should be checked and if necessary be re-set.

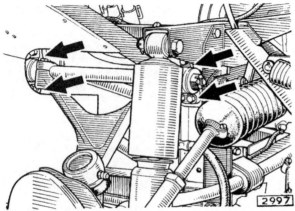

Fig. 75. The front wheel camber angle is adjusted by means of the shims indicated by arrows. Remove or add an equal number of shims from each position.

Front Wheel Castor Angle—Adjustment

Special links should be used when setting the castor angle of the front wheels. These links, which fit over the nuts of the top and bottom shock absorber mountings, hold the suspension in the mid-laden position. If the links are not available, additional weight should be added to the car to give a dimension of 13½ in. (34.28 cm.) between the centres of the shock absorber mountings which will be the mid-laden point of the front suspension.
Ensure that the tyre pressures are correct and that the car is standing on a level surface.
Using an approved gauge check the castor angle.
Castor angle. 2 deg. ± ½ deg. positive.

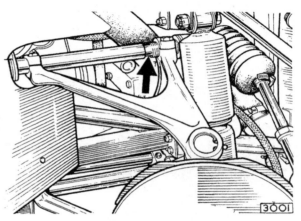

Fig. 76. The castor angle is adjusted by rotating the shaft indicated by the arrow.

Note: The castor angle for each wheel must not vary by more than ½ deg.
Adjustment is effected by rotating the round threaded shaft on the front suspension top wishbone bracket.

80

Remove split pins and release nuts situated at the front and rear of shaft and release wishbone bracket clamping bolts. Shaft may now be turned with spanner placed on the two flats provided on shaft.

Note: It is essential that split pins be removed and nuts released from shaft otherwise a strain will be placed on the rubber mounting bushes.

To increase positive castor angle rotate shaft anti-clockwise (viewed from front of car); to decrease castor angle rotate shaft clockwise.

After adjustment re-tighten clamp bolts (two) re-tighten nuts and fit split pins.

If any adjustment is made to the castor angle, the front wheel alignment should be checked and if necessary re-set.

The front of the car should be jacked up when turning the wheels from lock to lock during checking.

Front Wheel Bearings

Removal of the wheels will expose a grease nipple in the wheel bearing hubs. Lubricate sparingly with the recommended grade of lubricant. If excess grease is pumped into the bearing hubs the grease will exude into the bore of the splined hubs.

Always thoroughly clean the grease nipple before applying the grease gun.

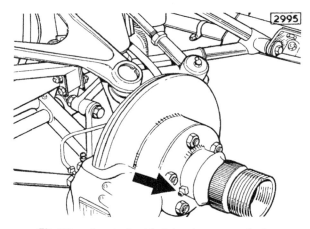

Fig. 77.   Front wheel hub bearing grease nipple.

81

REAR SUSPENSION

Rear Shock Absorbers

The rear shock absorbers are telescopic and contain no provision for replenishment of fluid.

Outer Pivot Bearings

A grease nipple is located in the centre of the rear wishbone outer pivot. Lubricate sparingly with the recommended grade of lubricant. A bleed hole is provided, opposite the grease nipple, to indicate when an excess of lubricant has been applied. Always ascertain that the bleed hole is clear before carrying out operation.

Inner Pivot Bearing

Two grease nipples are provided located at either end of the wishbone fork. Lubricate sparingly with the recommended grade of lubricant.

Half Shafts

Lubricate the universal joints of the half shafts (4 per car) with the recommended grade of lubricant. Access to the nipples of the outer joints is gained by removing the plastic sealing plug from each outer joint cover.

Rear Wheel Bearings

A hole in the hub bearing housing for lubrication of the wheel bearings is accessible after removal of the wheel. Clean off the area around the dust cap to ensure that no dirt enters the hub. Prise out the cap and inject the recommended grade of grease through

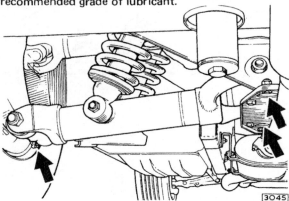

Fig. 78.   Outer and inner pivot bearing grease nipples.

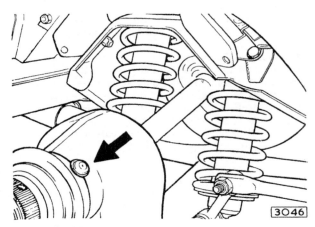

Fig. 79.   Rear wheel hub bearing grease cap.

the hole until no more will enter. If a pressure gun is used take care not to build-up pressure in the hub as the grease may escape past the oil seal. Refit the dust cap.

Rear Wheel Camber Angle—Adjustment

Owing to the variations in camber angle with different suspension heights, it is necessary to lock the rear suspension in the mid-laden position by means of two setting links. These links fit over the hub carrier fulcrum nut and hook into the lower hole of the rear mounting. If the links are not available, place weights in the boot of the car to load the suspension so that a dimension taken from the lower hole of the rear mounting to the centre of the hub carrier fulcrum nut is 8 3/16 in. (20.79 cm.). This will be the mid-laden point of the rear suspension.

Ensure that the car tyre pressures are correct and that the car is standing on level ground. Roll the car forward three lengths. Using an approved gauge check the camber angle.

Camber angle. ¾ deg. $\pm$ ¼ deg. negative.

Roll car forward 3 lengths and re-check.

Note: The camber angle for each wheel must not vary by more than ¼ deg.

Adjustment is effected by removing or adding shims between rear half shaft inboard universal joint and brake disc.

To adjust proceed as follows:—

Jack up the car and remove wheel being checked. Remove the four bolts and nuts securing the rear half shaft universal joint flange to the brake disc. Break away joint and add or subtract shims as necessary.

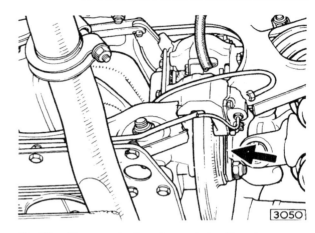

Fig. 80. The rear wheel camber angle is adjusted by means of shims indicated by the arrow.

Refit joint and fully tighten bolts and nuts. Adjust other wheel in a similar manner. Refit and lower wheels and remove jack.

Roll car forward 3 lengths and re-check camber angle. It should be noted that one shim 0.020 in. (0.5 mm.) will alter camber angle by approximately ¼ deg.

BRAKING SYSTEM

Brake Fluid Level

On right-hand drive cars the fluid reservoirs (two) for the hydraulic brakes are attached to the bulkhead.

On left-hand drive cars the fluid reservoirs (two) for the hydraulic brakes are attached adjacent to the exhaust manifold.

The reservoir to the master cylinder feeds the front brakes and the reservoir to the servo feeds the rear brakes.

At the recommended intervals check the level of fluid in the reservoirs and top up if necessary to the level mark, above fixing strap, marked "Fluid Level" using

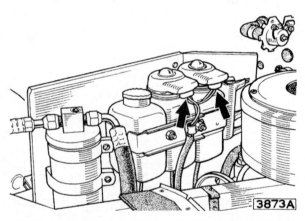

Fig. 81.   Brake fluid reservoirs—left-hand drive illustrated.

only the correct specification of Brake Fluid.

Do NOT overfill.

The level can be plainly seen through the plastic reservoir container.

First, disconnect the two electrical cables from the "snap-on" terminals. Unscrew the filler cap and "top-up" if necessary to the recommended level.

Insert the combined filler cap and float slowly into the reservoir to allow for displacement of fluid and screw down the cap. Wipe off any fluid from the top of the cap and connect the cables to either of the two terminals.

A further indication that the fluid level is becoming low is provided by an indicator pin situated between the two terminals.

First press down the pin and allow it to return to its normal position; if the pin can then be lifted with the thumb and forefinger the reservoir requires topping-up immediately.

Note: If it is found that the fluid level falls rapidly indicating a leak from the system, the car should be taken immediately to the nearest Jaguar Dealer for examination.

Footbrake Adjustment

Both the front wheel and rear wheel brakes are so designed that no manual adjustment to compensate for brake friction pad wear is necessary as this automatically takes place when the footbrake is applied.

Handbrake Mechanism

The mechanically operated handbrakes are attached to the rear caliper bodies but form an independent mechanically actuated system carrying its own friction pads. The hadbrakes are self adjusting to compensate for friction pad wear and automatically provide the necessary clearance between the friction pads and the discs.

If the travel of the handbrake level is excessive the handbrake cable should be adjusted as follows:—

Handbrake Cable Adjustment

Fully release the handbrake lever in the car. Slacken the locknut at the rear end of the handbrake cable.

Adjust the length of the cable by screwing out the threaded adaptor to a point just short of where the handbrake operating levers at the calipers start to move. Check the adjustment by pressing each operating lever at the same time towards the caliper; if any appreciable movement of the compensator linkage takes place the cable is too tight.

When correctly adjusted a certain amount of slackness will be apparent in the cable; no attempt should be made to place the cable under tension or the handbrakes may bind.

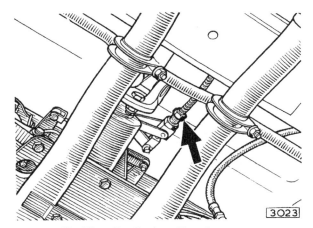

Fig. 82.   Handbrake cable adjustment.

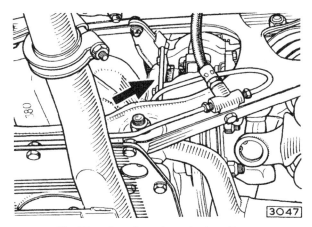

Fig. 83.   Location of rear brake calipers.

Friction Pads—Examination for Wear

At the recommended intervals, or if a loss of braking efficiency is noticed, the brake friction pads (2 per brake) should be examined for wear; the ends of the pads can be easily observed through the apertures in the brake caliper. When the friction pads have worn down to a thickness of approximately 1/8 in. (3.2 mm.) they need renewing.

Friction Pads—Renewal

To remove the friction pads, withdraw the hairpin clips and extract the anti-chatter clips and the pad retaining pins. Note that anti-chatter clips are only fitted on front calipers.

Lift the pads out of the caliper.

Push the pistons with an even pressure to the bottom of the cylinder bores and insert the new pads.

Replace the pad retaining pins and anti-chatter clips and secure with the hairpin clips.

Brake Fluid—Renewal

Connect rubber tubes to the bleed nipples on all calipers and insert the tubes into suitable containers. Release the bleed nipples one complete turn and expel the fluid by depressing the pedal and allowing it to return without assistance.

Repeat with a pause between each operation until no more fluid can be expelled.

Retract the pistons in the calipers and gently depress the pedal to remove any remaining fluid.

Fill the master cylinder reservoirs with Girling Cleaning Fluid and flush the system by repeating the draining operation.

Ensure that all Cleaning Fluid has been bled off; refill the reservoirs with the recommended grade of brake fluid and bleed the system.

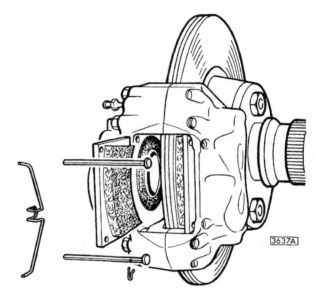

Fig. 84.   Friction pad renewal.

86

Bleeding the Brake Hydraulic System

"Bleeding" the brake hydraulic system (expelling the air) is not a routine maintenance operation and should only be necessary when a portion of the hydraulic system has been disconnected or if the level of the fluid has been allowed to fall.

The presence of air in the hydraulic system will cause the brakes to feel "spongy".

During the bleeding operation it is important that the level in the appropriate reservoir is kept topped up to avoid drawing air into the system.

1. Check that all the connections are tightened and all bleed screws closed.
2. Fill the appropriate reservoir with brake fluid of the correct specification.
3. Attach the bleeder tube to the bleed screw on the left-hand rear brake and immerse the open end of the tube in a small quantity of brake fluid contained in a clean glass jar. Slacken the bleed screw and operate the brake pedal slowly backwards and forwards through its full stroke until fluid pumped into the jar is reasonably free from air bubbles. Keep the pedal depressed and close the bleed screw. Release the brake pedal.
4. Repeat for right-hand rear brake.
   Repeat operation for front brakes.
5. Repeat the complete bleeding sequence until the brake fluid pumped into the jar is completely free from air bubbles.
6. Lock all bleed screws and finally regulate the fluid level in the reservoir.

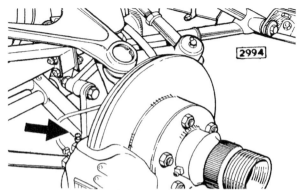

Fig. 85. Brake bleed nipple (front).

7. Apply normal working load on the brake pedal for a period of two or three minutes and examine the entire system for leaks.

Do not use the fluid which has been bled through the system to replenish the reservoir as it will have become aerated. Always use fresh fluid straight from the tin. Use only the recommended fluid.

Brake System — Overhaul

At the recommended intervals the brake system should be completely overhauled.

This important service should be entrusted to your Jaguar Dealer.

Brake Pipes — Checking

Check all pipes in the brake system at the commencement and end of each winter period for possible corrosion due to salt and grit used on the roads.

WHEEL AND TYRES

Tyre Pressures

It is important to maintain the tyre pressures at the correct figures given on page x of this book.

Incorrect pressures will affect the steering, riding comfort and tyre wear.

Check the inflation pressures when the tyres are cold and not when they have attained their normal running temperature; tyre pressures increase with driving and any such increase should be ignored.

Always ensure that the caps are fitted to the ends of the valves as they prevent the ingress of dirt and form a secondary seal to the valve core.

Tyre Replacement and Wheel Interchanging

When replacement of the rear tyres becomes necessary, fit new tyres to the existing rear wheels and, after balancing, fit these wheels to the front wheel positions on the car, fitting the existing front wheel and tyre assemblies (which should have useful tread life left) to the rear wheel positions on the car. If at the time this operation is carried out the tyre of the spare wheel is in new condition, it can be fitted to one of the front wheel positions in preference to replacing one of the original rear tyres, which wheel and tyre then become the spare.

Note: Due to the change in the steering characteristics which can be introduced by fitting to the front wheel positions wheels and tyres which have been used on the rear wheel positions, interchanging of part worn tyres from rear to front wheel positions is not recommended.

COACHWORK

Door Drain Holes
Clear the drain holes in the bottom of the doors with a piece of stiff wire.

Carpets
These may be cleaned by brushing or with a vacuum cleaner. Grease or oil stains can be removed with petrol.

Chromium Plate
Whilst all chrome-plated parts used on Jaguar cars are produced to a high standard, owners should note that deterioration of the plate may occur unless regular maintenance treatment is given.

With cars that are washed frequently and not operated in areas where climatic conditions liable to effect chrome plate exist, normal washing and leathering of the chrome and occasional use of chrome polish will maintain the plate in satisfactory condition.

In certain industrial areas or coastal areas, however, discolouration of the chrome plate from deposits in the atmosphere is liable to occur and more frequent attention is required.

Particular attention is drawn to the fact that salt is now commonly used on roads for frost or snow dispersal and it is of great importance that in areas where this treatment is used cars should be washed off as quickly as possible following use under these conditions.

Hood—Open 2 Seater
When cleaning the hood material care must be taken not to destroy the water-proofing qualities. Cleaning may be carried out with a soft brush and a "frothy" solution of a neutral soap and water. Stains may be removed by rubbing lightly with a white cloth moistened in methylated spirits.

Do not rub the plastic rear window with a dry cloth. Wash with soap and water only and rinse with clean water; dry with a soft cloth or sponge.

Head Lining
Dirt may be removed from the lining by the use of a vacuum cleaner. Stains may be removed by means of a white cloth moistened with methylated spirit applied briskly but without pressure.

Paintwork
Never clean the paintwork other than by washing with a soft sponge and hose pipe. Use a steady flow of water and sponge lightly. Dry and polish the paintwork with a good quality wash leather. Tar may be removed with a clean soft cloth moistened with petrol or with a proprietary brand of tar remover.

The paintwork may be polished from time to time with a good quality proprietary polish, either wax or emulsion type.

Upholstery
The leather should be wiped over occasionally with a cloth damped in warm soapy water. Repeat operation using fresh cloth and water alone (avoid flooding the leather) and finish by drying and polishing with a soft dry cloth. It is important to use a mild, non-caustic soap of the toilet kind and to avoid the use of petrol and detergents.

89

OIL CAN LUBRICATION

At the recommended intervals carry out oil can lubrication of the following points:

Seat runner and adjusting mechanism.
Handbrake lever ratchet.
Door locks.

Luggage compartment hinges and catches.
Bonnet hinges and catches.
Windscreen wiper arms.
Accelerator and carburetter linkage.
Fuel filler cover hinge.

ELECTRICAL EQUIPMENT

Battery Electrolyte Level
Under extremely cold conditions the battery should be topped up immediately prior to driving the vehicle so that electrolyte mixing can occur to prevent freezing of the added water.

This battery is fitted with an air-lock device. When topping up, the vehicle should be on a reasonably level surface.

Remove the vent cover. If the acid level is below the bottom of the tubes, pour distilled water into the trough until all tubes are filled.

Replace the vent cover. The electrolyte level is now correct.

Important: The vent cover must be kept in position at all times except when topping up. DO NOT use a Lucas Battery Filler for topping up.

Battery Connections
At the time of checking the electrolyte level ensure that battery terminals are clean and tight: if corroded, clean the insides of the terminals and smear with petroleum jelly.

IMPORTANT
These cars have a Negative Earth (ground) system and certain of the electrical components are different to those fitted to positive earth cars. When fitting auxiliary equipment or replacing any of the electrical components use only those specified for this particular model or ensure that they are suitable for use with negative earth.

Fuses

Should a component in the electrical system fail to function it is possible that the fuse protecting that component has blown.

Should a replacement fuse of the correct type also blow this indicates a fault in the circuit serving the affected component, and the car should therefore be taken to the nearest Jaguar dealer for examination.

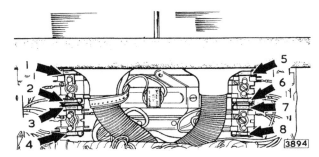

Fig. 86.   Location of fuses.

The fuses are located behind the instrument panel and access to them is obtained by removing the two instrument panel retaining screws (top left-hand and right-hand corners). The instrument panel will now hinge downwards exposing fuses and fuse indicator plate.

Circuits controlled by individual fuses are shown on the indicator plate and spare fuses are provided. It is essential that a blown fuse is replaced by one of the correct value.

A 15 amp. in-line fuse is incorporated in the circuit of the electrically heated backlight and is located below the fuse block behind the instrument panel.

Always replace spare fuse as soon as possible.

Fuse No.	Circuits	Amps
1	Headlamp (main beam) . . .	35
2	Headlamp (dip beam)	35
3	Horns	50
4	Traffic hazard warning device (if fitted)	35
5	Side, tail, panel, number plate lamps	35
6	Horn relay, washer, radiator fan motors, stop lamps	35
7	Flasher, heater, wiper, choke, fuel, water, oil gauges	35
8	Head lamp flash, interior lamps, cigar lighter	35
—	Electrically heated backlight (optional extra)	15

Headlamp Beam Setting

The alignment of the headlamp beams is set correctly before the car leaves the factory but if for any reason adjustment becomes necessary the following instructions should be carried out.

Place the car on a level surface in front of a garage door or wall; the car should be at least 25 feet (7.6 m.) away and square to the door or wall. Carry out the work with conditions as dark as possible so that the oval shaped light areas can be seen clearly.

With the headlamps in the full beam positions, that is, not dipped, the beams from the two headlamps should be parallel with the ground and with each other; measurements should be taken from the centres of the headlamps and the horizontal and vertical axes of the oval light areas. If adjustment is required remove the headlamp rim (retained by spring clips). Switch on headlamps and check that the beams are not in the dipped position.

The setting of the beams are adjusted by two screws. The top screw 'A' is the vertical adjustment, that is, to raise or lower the beam; turn the screw anti-clockwise to lower the beam and clockwise to raise the beam.

The side screw 'B' is for side adjustment. That is, to turn the beam to right or left. To move the beam to the right turn the screw clockwise. To move the beam to the left turn the screw anti-clockwise.

Headlamp Unit—Replacement

Remove the headlamp unit by inserting a screwdriver behind the rim at the rear edge and prising off. (The rim is retained by spring clips).

Remove the three cross-headed screws and detach the retaining ring.

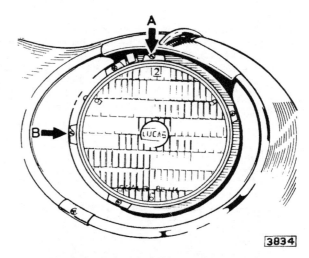

Fig. 87.   Adjustment of the screw 'A' will alter the headlamp beams in the vertical plane; adjustment of the screw 'B' will alter the beam in the horizontal plane.

Note: Do not disturb the two slotted screws or the setting of the headlamp will be upset.

Withdraw the light unit and unplug the adaptor.

Replace with a sealed beam unit of the correct type (see "Lamp Bulbs" page 12).

On cars fitted with non-sealed beam units, proceed as described above until the unit is removed, release the spring retaining clips and withdraw the bulb.

Replace with a bulb of the correct type (see "Lamp Bulbs" page 12). When re-assembling note that a groove in the bulb plate must register with a raised portion on the bulb retainer.

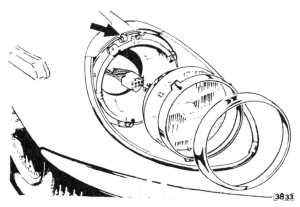

Fig. 88.   Headlamp bulb removal. The arrow indicates one of the spring clips retaining the rim.

Sidelamp Bulb—Replacement

Remove three screws retaining lamp glass and remove glass. The side lamb bulb is the outer one of the two exposed and is removed by pressing inwards and rotating anti-clockwise.

Front Flasher Bulb—Replacement

Proceed as for sidelamp bulb. The flasher bulb is the inner one of the two exposed.

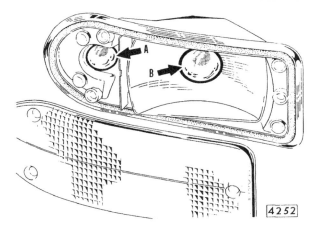

Fig. 89.   A—Sidelamp bulb.
B—Flasher bulb.

Rear/Brake Bulb—Replacement

Remove the four screws retaining lamp glass and remove glass. The rear/braking light bulb is the lower one of the two bulbs exposed and is removed by pressing inwards and rotating anti-clockwise. When fitting a replacement bulb note that the pins are offset.

Rear Flasher Bulb—Replacement

Proceed as for rear/brake lamp bulb. The flasher bulb is the top one of the two exposed.

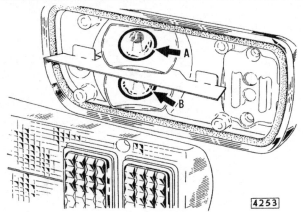

Fig. 90.   A—Rear flasher bulb.
           B—Rear/brake bulb.

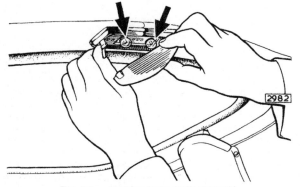

Fig. 91.   Interior lamp bulb removal.

Interior Lamp Bulb—Replacement (F.H. Coupe and 2 + 2)

Release the spring side clip and withdraw the retaining tongue on the glass cover from the slot in the lamp base.

To remove either bulb, press in and rotate anti-clockwise.

When refitting, ensure that the retaining tongue is correctly inserted in the slot in the base before locking in position.

Interior/Luggage Lamp Bulb—Replacement (Open 2-seater)

The Interior/Luggage lamp bulb is retained in a holder accessible when the boot lid is raised. To remove bulb from its holder press in and rotate anti-clockwise.

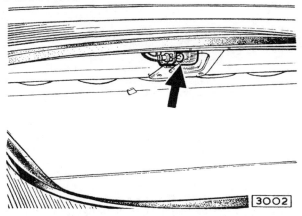

Fig. 92.   Interior lamp bulb removal (Open 2 seater).

Number Plate Lamp Bulb—Replacement

Remove the two screws retaining the lamp glass and detach the glass and chrome rim. Remove either bulb by pressing and rotating in an anti-clockwise direction.

Traffic Hazard Indicator Bulb—Replacement

Remove the chrome bezel and unscrew the bulb from the bulb holder.

Backlight Heater Indicator Bulb—Replacement

Remove the chrome bezel and unscrew the bulb from the bulb holder.

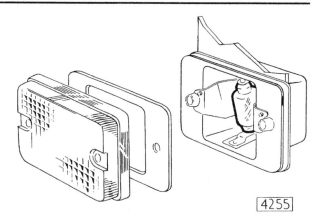

Fig. 94.   Reverse lamp bulb removal.

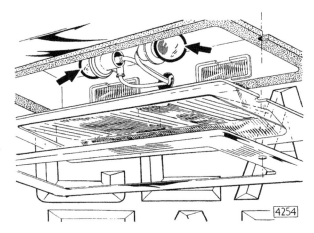

Fig. 93.   Number plate lamp bulb removal.

Reverse Lamp Bulb—Replacement

Remove fixing screws retaining rim to lamp glass and detach glass and gasket. To remove the bulb, lift the upper contact and withdraw the bulb.

Automatic Transmission Indicator Bulb—Replacement (2 + 2)

Remove the drive screws and detach the arm rest and transmission unit tunnel cover.
Unscrew the gear control knob.
Withdraw two screws and detach the gear indicator cover.
Detach the bulb cover and withdraw the bulb.
Replace the bulb with one of the correct voltage (24 volts).

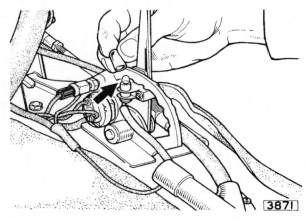

Fig. 95.   Automatic transmission indicator bulb removal.

Electric Clock—Battery Renewal (Early Cars)

The electric clock is a fully transistorised instrument powered by a small dry battery.

The battery is contained in a plastic holder attached to the back of the clock. Renew the battery every 18 months to maintain perfect time-keeping.

To renew, unscrew the instrument panel retaining screws and hinge down the panel. Lever the battery out of the holder. Press the new battery into the holder. Refit the instrument panel.

Fig. 96.   Renewing electric clock battery.

ROUTINE MAINTENANCE

DAILY
Check engine oil level.
Check coolant level.

WEEKLY
Check battery electrolyte level.
Check tyre pressures.
Check water level in screen washer bottle.

3,000 Miles (5,000 Km.) CHECK SERVICE

1. Check oil or fluid levels and top up as necessary:—
    - (a) Engine sump,
    - (b) Brake reservoirs,
    - (c) Clutch reservoir (if fitted),
    - (d) Power steering reservoir (if fitted),
    - (e) Top up carburetter hydraulic dampers and check carburation,
    - (f) Battery,
    - (g) Screen washer bottle,
    - (h) Radiator header tank (add anti-freeze when necessary),
    - (i) Manual gearbox,
    - (j) Final drive unit.
2. Check driving belts for correct tension.
3. Examine brake pads for wear & check operation of brake stop lights.
4. Examine tyres for damage and adjust pressures.
5. Check tightness of road wheel nuts.

Repeat at:—

Miles	Kilometres
9,000	15,000
15,000	25,000
21,000	35,000
27,000	45,000
33,000	55,000
39,000	65,000
45,000	75,000
51,000	85,000
57,000	95,000
63,000	105,000
69,000	115,000

6,000 Miles (10,000 Km.) MINOR SERVICE

1. Check oil or fluid levels and top up as necessary:—
    - (a) Brake reservoirs,
    - (b) Clutch reservoir (if fitted),
    - (c) Power steering reservoir (if fitted),
    - (d) Top up carburetter dampers,
    - (e) Battery and check connections,
    - (f) Screen washer bottle,
    - (g) Radiator header tank (add anti-freeze when necessary),
    - (h) Manual gearbox or automatic transmission unit,
    - (i) Final drive unit.
2. Drain and refill:—
    - (a) Engine sump. Fit new oil filter element and seal.
3. Check driving belts for correct tension.
4. Check brake pads for wear and advise wear-rate to owner.

Repeat at:—

Miles	Kilometres
18,000	30,000
30,000	50,000
42,000	70,000
54,000	90,000
66,000	110,000

12,000 Miles (20,000 Km.) MAJOR SERVICE

1. Check oil or fluid levels and top up as necessary: —
   - (a) Brake reservoirs,
   - (b) Clutch reservoir (if fitted),
   - (c) Power steering reservoir (if fitted),
   - (d) Top up carburetter hydraulic dampers,
   - (e) Battery and check connections,
   - (f) Screen washer bottle,
   - (g) Radiator header tank (add anti-freeze when necessary),
   - (h) Automatic transmission,
   - (i) Final drive unit.

2. Drain and refill : —
   - (a) Engine Sump. Fit new oil filter element and seal.
   - (b) Manual gearbox. Clean overdrive filter (if fitted),
   - (c) Final drive unit (Powr-Lok differential if fitted — use only special limited slip oil.

3. Renew Sparking plugs.
4. Renew Air cleaner element and fuel line filter element.
5. Clean and adjust contact breaker points. Check operation of centrifugal advance mechanism. Lubricate distributor.
6. Check driving belts for wear and tension.
7. Adjust top timing chain if required.
8. Lubricate all grease nipples including front and rear wheel bearings.
9. Check all suspension and exhaust mountings for security.
10. Check all steering connections, ball joints etc., for security and wear.
11. Check brake pads for degree of wear and advise wear-rate to owner.
12. Check functioning of all mandatory lights including stop lights and alignment of headlamps.
13. Check tyres for damage and tread depth. If uneven wear evident, check wheel alignment. Adjust pressures.
14. Oil can lubrication of door locks, bonnet hinges and locks, boot hinges and lock, seat slides, fuel filler flap hinges, control linkages.
15. Detect and report any oil, petrol, water, hydraulic fluid leakage and damaged hoses or other damaged parts.

Repeat at: —

Miles	Kilometres
24,000	40,000
48,000	80,000
60,000	100,000

24,000 Miles (40,000 Km.) ADDITIONAL SERVICE

1. Brake system. Drain off old fluid, retract wheel pistons on wheel cylinders to complete operation.
   Flush out system, and refill with new fluid.

48,000 Miles (80,000 Km.) ADDITIONAL SERVICE

1. Overhaul complete brake system.

98

36,000 Miles (60,000 Km.) MAJOR SERVICE

1. Check oil or fluid levels and top up as necessary:—
   - (a)   Clutch reservoir (if fitted),
   - (b)   Power steering reservoir (if fitted),
   - (c)   Top up carburetter hydraulic dampers,
   - (d)   Battery and check connections,
   - (e)   Screen washer bottle,
   - (f)   Radiator header tank (add anti-freeze when necessary),
   - (g)   Automatic transmission,
   - (h)   Final drive unit.
2. Drain and refill:—
   - (a)   Engine sump. Fit new oil filter element and seal,
   - (b)   Manual gearbox. Clean overdrive filter (if fitted),
   - (c)   Braking system. Retract, wheel cylinder pistons to expel all old fluid,
   - (d)   Final drive unit (Powr-Lok differential if fitted—use only special limited slip oil).
3. Renew Sparking plugs.
4. Renew Air cleaner element and fuel line filter element.
5. Clean and adjust contact breaker points. Check operation of centrifugal advance mechanism. Lubricate distributor.
6. Check driving belts for wear and tension.
7. Adjust top timing chain if required.
8. Lubricate all grease nipples including front and rear wheel bearings.
9. Check all suspension and exhaust mountings for security.
10. Check all steering connections, ball joints etc., for security and wear.
11. Check brake pads for degree of wear and advise wear-rate to owner.
12. Check functioning of all mandatory lights including stop lights and alignment of headlamps.
13. Check tyres for damage and tread depth. If uneven wear evident, check wheel alignment. Adjust pressures.
14. Oil can lubrication of door locks, bonnet hinges and locks, boot hinges and lock, seat slides, fuel filler flap hinges, control linkages.
15. Detect and report any oil, petrol, water, hydraulic fluid leakage and damaged hoses or other damaged parts.

Repeat at:—

Miles	Kilometres
72,000	120,000

IMPORTANT

If the car is fitted with Stromberg 175CD 2SE carburetters (U.S.A. only) consult your Jaguar Dealer for all Routine Maintenance Service concerning Engine Emission Control. Tuning by unqualified persons must NOT be attempted.

RECOMMENDED LUBRICANTS

Component	Mobil	Castrol	Shell	Esso	B.P.	Duck-ham	Texaco
Engine	Mobil Super or Mobil Special	Castrol GTX	Shell Super Oil	Uniflow	Super Visco-Static 10W/40	Q20/50 or Q5500	Havoline 20W/50 or 10W/30
Upper cylinder Lubrication	Mobil Upper-lube	Castrollo	Shell U.C.L. or Donax U	Esso U.C.L.	Energol U.C.L.	Adcoid Liquid	Texaco U.C.L.
Distributor oil can points Oil can lubrication	Mobiloil A	Castrol GTX	Shell Super Oil	Uniflow	Energol SAE 30	Q20-50	Havoline 30
Final drive unit (not 'Powr-Lok') Gearbox	Mobilube GX 90	Castrol Hypoy	Spirax 90 EP	Esso Gear Oil GX 90/140	Gear Oil SAE 90 EP	Hypoid 90	Universal Lubricant 90
Front wheel bearings Rear wheel bearings Distributor cam Rear Suspension Final drive half-shafts Steering tie-rods Wheel swivels Door hinges Steering rack housing	Mobil-grease MP	Castrol-ease LM	Retinax A	Esso Multi-purpose grease H	Ener-grease L.2	LB 10	Marfak All purpose
Automatic transmission unit Power-steering	Mobil ATF.201	Castrol T.Q.F.	Shell Donax T7	Esso Glide	BP Autran B	Q-matic	Texa-matic 6691

RECOMMENDED HYDRAULIC FLUID

Braking System and Clutch Operation

Castrol/Girling Crimson Clutch/Brake Fluid is recommended. This conforms to SAE J1703A specification but has a higher boiling point for additional safety. Where Castrol/Girling Crimson is not available, only fluid guaranteed to conform to SAE J1703A specification may be used as an alternative.

TYRE PRESSURES

Check pressures with the tyres cold and not when they have attained
their normal running temperature.

Type: DUNLOP SP SPORT

185VR15

Pressures	Front	Rear
For speeds up to 125 m.p.h. (200 k.p.h.)	32 lb./sq. in. (2.25 kg./sq. cm.)	32 lb./sq. in. (2.25 kg./sq. cm.)
For speeds up to maximum *(Countries with no speed limitation)*	40 lb./sq. in. (2.81 kg./sq. cm.)	40 lb./sq. in. (2.81 kg./sq. cm.)

DUNLOP WEATHERMASTER SP44.185x15

(when snow conditions make the use of special tyres necessary)
Always use special inner tube — see Handbook

(For use only on rear wheels to replace SP. Sport tyres) . . . . 32 lb./sq. in.
(2.25 kg./sq. cm.)

Maximum permitted speed 100 m.p.h. (160 k.p.h.).

CAPACITIES

	Imperial pints	U.S. pints	Litres
Engine (refill including filter)	15	18	8.5
Gearbox (Early cars)	2½	3	1.42
Gearbox (Later cars)	3	3¾	2.4
Automatic transmission unit from dry (2+2 only) . .	16	19	9
Final Drive Unit	2¾	3¼	1.54
Cooling system (including heater)	27	32 1/5	15.36

	Imperial gallons	U.S. gallons	Litres
Petrol tank	14	16¾	63.64

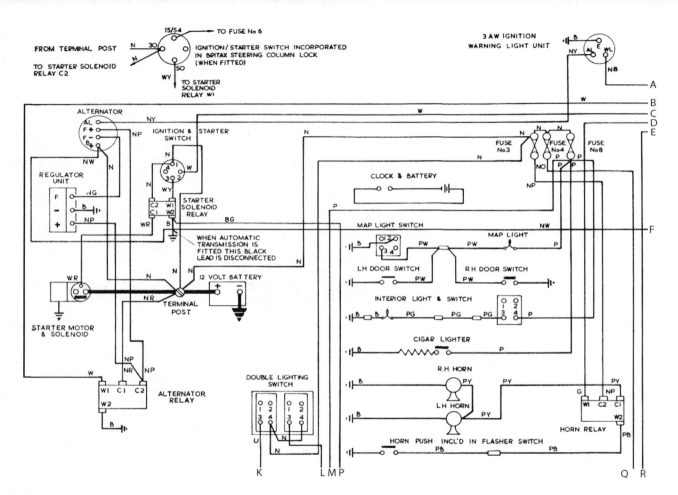

FROM TERMINAL POST

TO STARTER SOLENOID RELAY C2

15/54 — TO FUSE No 6

IGNITION/STARTER SWITCH INCORPORATED IN BRITAX STEERING COLUMN LOCK (WHEN FITTED)

TO STARTER SOLENOID RELAY W1

3 AW IGNITION WARNING LIGHT UNIT

ALTERNATOR

IGNITION & STARTER SWITCH

REGULATOR UNIT

STARTER SOLENOID RELAY

WHEN AUTOMATIC TRANSMISSION IS FITTED THIS BLACK LEAD IS DISCONNECTED

STARTER MOTOR & SOLENOID

TERMINAL POST

12 VOLT BATTERY

ALTERNATOR RELAY

DOUBLE LIGHTING SWITCH

FUSE No3   FUSE No4   FUSE No8

CLOCK & BATTERY

MAP LIGHT SWITCH   MAP LIGHT

LH DOOR SWITCH   R H DOOR SWITCH

INTERIOR LIGHT & SWITCH

CIGAR LIGHTER

R.H. HORN

LH HORN

HORN PUSH INCL'D IN FLASHER SWITCH

HORN RELAY

102

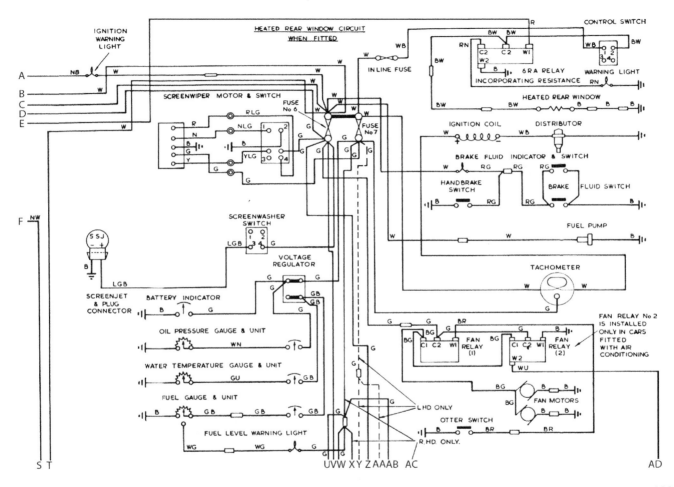

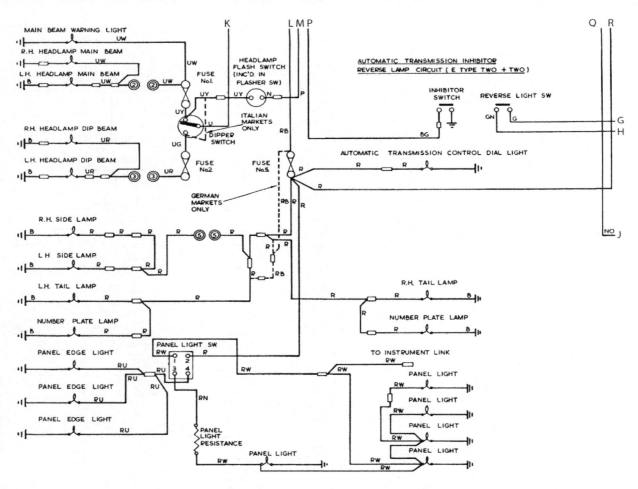

MAIN BEAM WARNING LIGHT

R.H. HEADLAMP MAIN BEAM

L.H. HEADLAMP MAIN BEAM

FUSE No.1.

HEADLAMP FLASH SWITCH (INC'D. IN FLASHER SW)

DIPPER SWITCH

ITALIAN MARKETS ONLY

AUTOMATIC TRANSMISSION INHIBITOR
REVERSE LAMP CIRCUIT (E TYPE TWO + TWO)

INHIBITOR SWITCH

REVERSE LIGHT SW

R.H. HEADLAMP DIP BEAM

L.H. HEADLAMP DIP BEAM

FUSE No2.

GERMAN MARKETS ONLY

FUSE No.5.

AUTOMATIC TRANSMISSION CONTROL DIAL LIGHT

R.H. SIDE LAMP

L.H SIDE LAMP

L.H. TAIL LAMP

NUMBER PLATE LAMP

R.H. TAIL LAMP

NUMBER PLATE LAMP

PANEL EDGE LIGHT

PANEL EDGE LIGHT

PANEL EDGE LIGHT

PANEL LIGHT SW.

TO INSTRUMENT LINK

PANEL LIGHT

PANEL LIGHT

PANEL LIGHT

PANEL LIGHT

PANEL
LIGHT
RESISTANCE

PANEL LIGHT

PANEL LIGHT

104

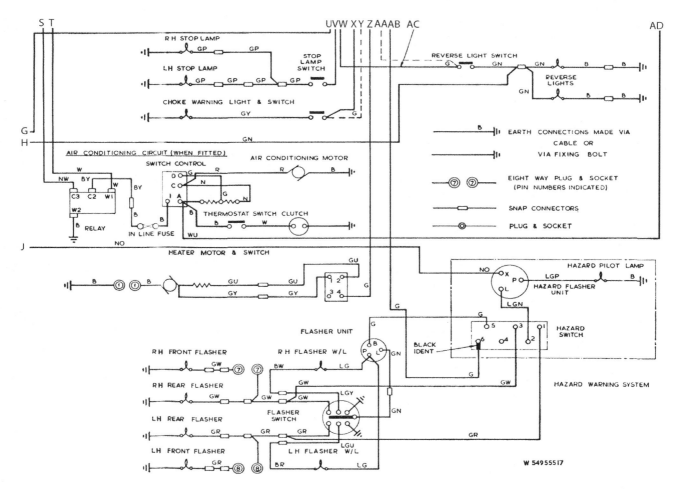

W 54955517

105

4.2 LITRE 'E' TYPE SERIES 2

CABLE
COLOUR CODE

B	BLACK	**S**	SLATE
U	BLUE	**W**	WHITE
N	BROWN	**Y**	YELLOW
R	RED	**D**	DARK
P	PURPLE	**L**	LIGHT
G	GREEN	**M**	MEDIUM

When a cable has two colour code letters, the first denotes the main colour and the second denotes the tracer colour.

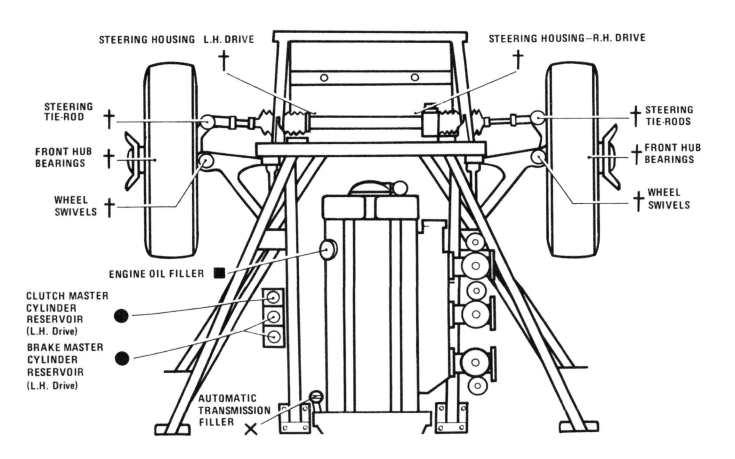

STEERING HOUSING L.H. DRIVE

STEERING HOUSING—R.H. DRIVE

STEERING
TIE-ROD

FRONT HUB
BEARINGS

WHEEL
SWIVELS

STEERING
TIE-RODS

FRONT HUB
BEARINGS

WHEEL
SWIVELS

ENGINE OIL FILLER

CLUTCH MASTER
CYLINDER
RESERVOIR
(L.H. Drive)

BRAKE MASTER
CYLINDER
RESERVOIR
(L.H. Drive)

AUTOMATIC
TRANSMISSION
FILLER

107

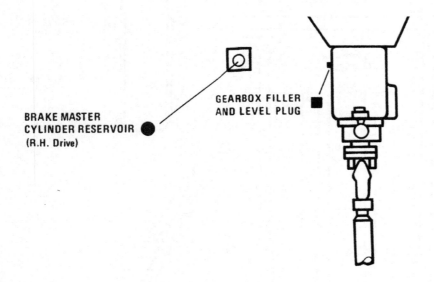

BRAKE MASTER CYLINDER RESERVOIR
(R.H. Drive)

GEARBOX FILLER AND LEVEL PLUG

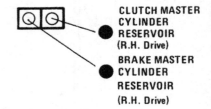

CLUTCH MASTER CYLINDER RESERVOIR
(R.H. Drive)

BRAKE MASTER CYLINDER RESERVOIR
(R.H. Drive)

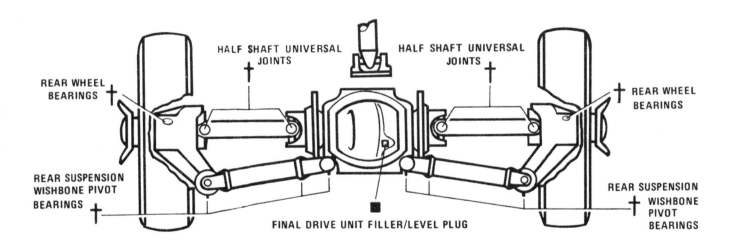

REAR WHEEL BEARINGS

HALF SHAFT UNIVERSAL JOINTS

HALF SHAFT UNIVERSAL JOINTS

REAR WHEEL BEARINGS

REAR SUSPENSION WISHBONE PIVOT BEARINGS

REAR SUSPENSION WISHBONE PIVOT BEARINGS

FINAL DRIVE UNIT FILLER/LEVEL PLUG

† GREASE

■ OIL

● BRAKE FLUID

✕ AUTOMATIC TRANSMISSION FLUID

DRAIN PLUGS

ENGINE

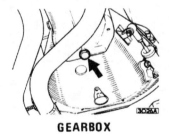

GEARBOX

FINAL DRIVE UNIT

OFFICIAL TECHNICAL BOOKS

Brooklands Technical Books has been formed to supply owners,
restorers and professional repairers with
official factory literature.

Workshop Manuals

Jaguar Service Manual 1946-1948		9781855207844
Jaguar XK 120 140 150 150S & Mk 7, 8 & 9		9781870642279
Jaguar Mk 2 (2.4 3.4 3.8 240 340)	E121/7	9781870642958
Jaguar Mk 10 (3.8 & 4.2) & 420G	E136/2	9781855200814
Jaguar 'S' Type 3.4 & 3.8	E133/3	9781870642095
Jaguar E-Type 3.8 & 4.2 Series 1 & 2		
E123/8, E123 B/3 & E156/1		9781855200203
Jaguar E-Type V12 Series 3	E165/3	9781855200012
Jaguar 420	E143/2	9781855201712
Jaguar XJ6 2.8 & 4.2 Series 1		9781855200562
Jaguar XJ6 3.4 & 4.2 Series	E188/4	9781855200302
Jaguar XJ12 Series 1		9781783180417
Jaguar XJ12 Series 2 / DD6 Series 2	E190/4	9781855201408
Jaguar XJ6 & XJ12 Series 3	AKM9006	9781855204010
Jaguar XJ6 OWM (XJ40) 1986-94		9781855207851
Jaguar XJS V12 5.3 & 6.0 Litre	AKM3455	9781855202627
Jaguar XJS 6 Cylinder 3.6 & 4.0 Litre	AKM9063	9781855204638

Owners Workshop Manuals

Jaguar E-Type V12 1971-1974	9781783181162
Jaguar XJ, Sovereign 1968-1982	9781783811179
Jaguar XJ6 Workshop Manual 1986-1994	9781855207851
Jaguar XJ12, XJ5.3 Double Six 1972-1979	9781783181186

Owners Handbooks

Jaguar XK120		9781855200432
Jaguar XK140	E101/2	9781855200401
Jaguar XK150	E111/2	9781855200395
Jaguar Mk 2 (3.4)	E116/10	9781855201682
Jaguar Mk 2 (3.8)	E115/10	9781869826765
Jaguar E-Type (Tuning & prep. for competition)		9781855207905
Jaguar E-Type 3.8 Series 1	E122/7	9781870642927
Jaguar E-Type 4.2 2+2 Series 1	E131/6	9781869826383
Jaguar E-Type 4.2 Series	E154/5	9781869826499
Jaguar E-Type V12 Series 3	E160/2	9781855200029
Jaguar E-Type V12 Series 3 (US)	A181/2	9781855200036
Jaguar XJ (3.4 & 4.2) Series 2	E200/8	9781855201200
Jaguar XJ6C Series 2	E184/1	9781855207875
Jaguar XJ12 Series 3	AKM4181	9781855207868

Carburetters

SU Carburetters Tuning Tips & Techniques	9781855202559
Solex Carburetters Tuning Tips & Techniques	9781855209770
Weber Carburettors Tuning Tips and Techniques	9781855207592

www.brooklandsbooks.com

Printed and distributed by Brooklands Books Ltd., PO Box 904,
Amersham, Bucks, HP6 9JA, England

Part Number: E.154/5

ISBN 9781869826499   Ref: J39HH   10W4/2992

Printed in Great Britain
by Amazon

56781912R00064